Catriona Neil | Adrian Spalding

111 Places
in Cornwall
That You
Shouldn't Miss

T0244020

emons:

Bibliographical information of the Deutsche Nationalbibliothek
The Deutsche Nationalbibliothek lists this publication in
the Deutsche Nationalbibliografie; detailed bibliographical data
are available on the internet at http://dnb.d-nb.de.

© Emons Verlag GmbH
All rights reserved
© Photographs by Adrian Spalding and Catriona Neil
Barbara Hepworth Museum (ch. 90): Barbara Hepworth *Spring*,
1966 © Bowness, photo by Adrian Spalding
King Arthur's Great Halls (ch. 97): "Arthur pulling the sword
from the anvil" by Veronica Whall, photo by Adrian Spalding
© Cover icon: istockphoto.com/Kneonlight
Layout: Eva Kraskes, based on a design
by Lübbeke | Naumann | Thoben
Maps: altancicek.design, www.altancicek.de
Basic cartographical information from Openstreetmap,
© OpenStreetMap-Mitwirkende, OdbL
Edited by: Tania Taylor
Printing and binding: Grafisches Centrum Cuno, Calbe
Printed in Germany 2024
ISBN 978-3-7408-1901-9
First edition

Guidebooks for Locals & Experienced Travellers
Join us in uncovering new places around the world at
www.111places.com

Foreword

Between us, we have lived in Cornwall for over 100 years, and yet in writing this book we found places and stories we knew nothing of. Here we give you a taste of its character beyond the famous features, then your curiosity will lead you further.

Cornwall, or Kernow as this land is known, is unique in Britain. It is a world with its own culture and language, a place where you are surrounded by prehistory sitting side by side with so much that is new. We hark back to the earliest inhabitants, who left intriguing fogous, quoits and standing stones; we pay homage to the tin miners and fishermen, men in those industries at the heart of Cornish identity – along with farming – all still alive but changing with the times: the importance of mining in shaping the landscape and economy cannot be ignored.

Coming forward in time, we visit the place from which the first global radio signal was sent across the Atlantic, and explore world-leading telecommunications and a deep space telecom enterprise.

The fierce will of the Cornish people to retain their identity is clear in Cornwall's battles and culture. So we include civil war backdrops, the great Cornish rebellion of 1497 and sites linked with the great wars of the 20th century.

We visit large gardens – splendid in the mild spring weather for which Cornwall is famous – and sites used in films, novels and television series. We celebrate great artists, the last native Cornish speaker, breathtaking wildlife, awe-inspiring geology and the transformative contribution of its sons to engineering and scientific innovations, notably the birth of the steam engine. We show you where to look at the stars, cross rivers by stepping stones, find places to eat, ride on steam railways, buy a deep-water diving bell, and even where a tiny village found itself in a dispute with a global fashion magazine over its name.

Catriona Neil and *Adrian Spalding*

111 Places

1 __ Pencarrow House
Snowdrops galore and Rosamunde Pilcher | 10

2 __ King Arthur's Hall
Worth the walk – if you can find it! | 12

3 __ Starling Roost
Startling starlings | 14

4 __ Temple Church
The house of the Knights Templar | 16

5 __ St Juliot Church
A pair of blue eyes | 18

6 __ Brenda Wootton
The Voice of Cornwall | 20

7 __ The Barge Tearoom
Tea afloat the only canal in Cornwall | 22

8 __ The Battle of Stamford Hill
Roundhead or Cavalier? | 24

9 __ Millook
Flat-packed rocks | 26

10 __ Dupath Well
Whoop, whoop, hurray | 28

11 __ Kit Hill
Look across to England and be happy you're in Cornwall | 30

12 __ Carn Brea Castle
Dine in granite on top of the hill | 32

13 __ National Dahlia Collection
Shall I eat it or just fall in love with its colours? | 34

14 __ Puffing Devil
Capn Dick's puffer | 36

15 __ Davidstow Moor RAF Memorial Museum
World War II Coastal Command, 970 feet up | 38

16 __ Poldice Copper Mine
Buddles and calciners | 40

17 __ Penjerrick Garden
Darwin's brain coral | 42

18 __ Royal Cornwall Polytechnic
The first polytechnic | 44

Sea Shanty Festival
For this is my Cornwall and this is my home | 46

Trebah Garden
Champion trees and Nessie's Cornish relative | 48

Ukraine Monument
A symbol of solidarity | 50

Bodinnick Ferry
Past Daphne du Maurier's Ferryside | 52

The Tristan Stone
The travelling stone | 54

Glow-worms at Gwithian Dunes
Green glows at night | 56

Frenchman's Creek
Marriage and piracy don't mix! | 58

Helford Ferry
Save your legs on the South West Coast Path | 60

Blue Anchor
600 years of Spingo Ale | 62

Bob Fitzsimmons
The bigger they are, the harder they fall | 64

Hal-an-Tow
Summer is a come, O! | 66

Museum of Cornish Life
Save a life for 20p | 68

Trelowarren Halliggye Fogou
Down into the dark; beware of spiders | 70

St Levan's Stone
When a pack horse can ride through St Levan's Stone | 72

Launceston Castle
The town's hard metaphor | 74

Launceston Steam Railway
Steam up along the Kensey Valley | 76

Zig Zag
As I went down Zig Zag | 78

Darley Oak
One thousand years old | 80

King Doniert's Stone
The last king of Cornwall | 82

Minions
Not those Minions | 84

Stuart House
King Charles slept here | 86

Goonhilly Earth Station
Who's there? | 88

Lizard Lighthouse
Pharology – the study of lighthouses | 90

Serpentine
Not the lake in London | 92

Britain's Most Southerly Café
Who's watching who? | 94

Giant's Hedge
The Devil's work? | 96

Lerryn Stepping Stones
Mind your step | 98

The Old Duchy Palace
Should tin miners pay tax? | 100

Mên Scryfa
Ancient stone with writing | 102

Hawker's Hut
The original man cave | 104

The Marconi Memorial
dit dit dit | 106

Laurence Binyon
At the going down of the sun | 108

The Fishermen Statue
When the fish are gone, what are the Cornish boys to do? | 110

Maen Cottage
Faraway Fancies | 112

Ordnance Datum
Looking at an OS map? Think of Newlyn | 114

The Huer's Hut
Heva, Heva now the catch is in, let the troyl begin | 116

Lappa Valley
Modern mining railway | 118

Doom Bar
Not the beer – the real thing! | 120

Prideaux Place
Padstow's Elizabethan manor | 122

Dolly Pentreath
My ny vynnav kewsel Sowsnek | 124

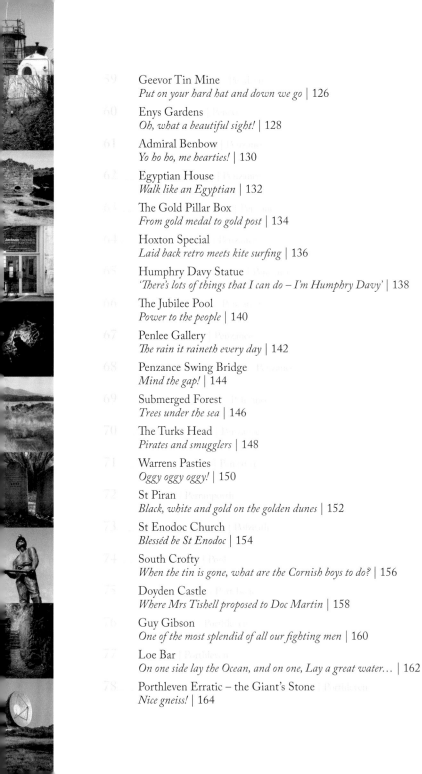

Geevor Tin Mine
Put on your hard hat and down we go | 126

Enys Gardens
Oh, what a beautiful sight! | 128

Admiral Benbow
Yo ho ho, me hearties! | 130

Egyptian House
Walk like an Egyptian | 132

The Gold Pillar Box
From gold medal to gold post | 134

Hoxton Special
Laid back retro meets kite surfing | 136

Humphry Davy Statue
'There's lots of things that I can do – I'm Humphry Davy' | 138

The Jubilee Pool
Power to the people | 140

Penlee Gallery
The rain it raineth every day | 142

Penzance Swing Bridge
Mind the gap! | 144

Submerged Forest
Trees under the sea | 146

The Turks Head
Pirates and smugglers | 148

Warrens Pasties
Oggy oggy oggy! | 150

St Piran
Black, white and gold on the golden dunes | 152

St Enodoc Church
Blesséd be St Enodoc | 154

South Crofty
When the tin is gone, what are the Cornish boys to do? | 156

Doyden Castle
Where Mrs Tishell proposed to Doc Martin | 158

Guy Gibson
One of the most splendid of all our fighting men | 160

Loe Bar
On one side lay the Ocean, and on one, Lay a great water… | 162

Porthleven Erratic – the Giant's Stone
Nice gneiss! | 164

79 Lady Bassett's Baths | Portreath
Hidden baths, surf and caves | 166

80 Macsalvors | Redruth
One stop shop for almost everything | 168

81 Wellie Dogs | Perranporth
Woof woof! | 170

82 The Ferryman Statue | Saltash
Ferry across the Tamar | 172

83 Seaton Beach | Seaton
Where the river Seaton meets the sea | 174

84 Lost Gardens of Heligan | St Austell
Shhhhhh! Don't wake her – or is it just a dream? | 176

85 Roche Rock | St Austell
Be careful how you ascend | 178

86 Treffry Viaduct | St Austell
Water 90 feet up | 180

87 Trevethy Quoit | St Cleer
Our quoit is bigger than yours | 182

88 Gwennap Pit | St Day
Hear a whisper | 184

89 Alfred Wallis | St Ives
Climbing the stairs to heaven | 186

90 Barbara Hepworth Museum | St Ives
Bronze sculpture in the garden | 188

91 St Ives Bay Railway | St Ives
The most scenic line in Britain? | 190

92 The Crowns Engine Houses | St Just
Lost in a card game in TV's Poldark | 192

93 Kurt Jackson Foundation | St Just
Best Art Gallery in Cornwall in the Muddy Stilettos Awards | 194

94 An Gof | St Keverne
A name perpetual | 196

95 Roskilly's | St Keverne
Proper Cornish – cream on top | 198

96 Japanese Garden | St Mawgan
Mossy green islands on gravel seas | 200

97 King Arthur's Great Halls | Tintagel
Our once and future king | 202

98 Cremyll Ferry | Torpoint
Cross the Tamar into Devon | 204

99   Cornwall's Dark Skies
Observatory for Cornwall | 206

100   The Drummer
A naked man! | 208

101   Joseph Antonio Emidy
Britain's first composer of the African diaspora | 210

102   Piero's
Ciao! | 212

103   The Red Lion
You don't know what you've got till it's gone | 214

104   Royal Cornwall Museum
From 6th-century stones to Lego | 216

105   Truro Cathedral
The very first Christmas Nine Lessons and Carols | 218

106   Truro Leats
Victorian plumbing | 220

107   Walsingham Place
Homes for mistresses | 222

108   The Bridge Over the Camel
The bridge built on wool | 224

109   St Breock Downs
The old and the new | 226

110   The Trevanion Culverhouse
Just popping into the medieval supermarket | 228

111   The Mermaid of Zennor
Then I will go with ye – for with ye is where I belong | 230

1 Pencarrow House
Snowdrops galore and Rosamunde Pilcher

Pencarrow House is a classic Georgian mansion, built in 1773, that sits on the edge of Bodmin Moor. For the Molesworth-St Aubyns this has been their family home for much of its 500-year history. The house is set in 50 acres of grounds, with grand lawns sweeping away from the front of the house towards the wilder wooded area, where there is an Iron Age fort known as Pencarrow Rounds. The remains of the fort are visible as a series of ramparts and ditches as you drive to the house.

There is plenty of interest here; as well as the hill fort there are many woodland walks and garden features including a sunken Italian Garden with elegant fountain, a hidden grotto, the first rockery garden in England (built with Bodmin Moor granite), the Memorial Garden summer display, an ice house, lake, a huge range of camellias and rhododendrons and, last but not least, free-roaming peacocks. The monkey puzzle tree (a 'marmite' species if ever there was one) is said to have got its name 100 years ago when the specimen at Pencarrow was planted, prompting one Charles Austin to comment that 'it would be a puzzle for a monkey'.

However, the thing that marks Pencarrow out for us is the truly delightful spring display of snowdrops, great drifts of purist white over the banks that surround the house, and bright little shining clusters in dark corners under sombre evergreens. The family generously opens the gardens at the height of the display to raise money for charity and it has to be one of the most uplifting sights on a dreary February day.

You can join a guided tour of the house, which is stunningly beautiful and has many interesting features. It has become famous as the setting for the Benson Valley Winery in the TV series of Rosamunde Pilcher's novel *English Wine* (*Englischer Wein*), and appears in *Doc Martin* and the *Fisherman's Friends* film.

Address Pencarrow, Bodmin, PL30 3AG, www.pencarrow.co.uk | **Getting there** House located on the A389 between Bodmin and Wadebridge (ignore your satnav); free parking | **Hours** Gardens open daily Apr–Oct 10am–5pm; check the website for house opening hours | **Tip** Nearby Bodmin has many historic features, most notably the jail and court room, mentioned in Winston Graham's *Poldark* novels.

2 King Arthur's Hall

Worth the walk – if you can find it!

Walk across the moor heading roughly north with the magnificent Rough Tor in the distance and you will find this curious rectangular enclosure, near the top of the rise, marked on each side by a low grassy bank. Now it is full of soft rush, with pools of water after heavy rain. But what was its original purpose? Is it a Neolithic feature? Did Stone Age man live here amongst the stone circles, hut circles, cairns and cists that surround the Hall, and perhaps hold ceremonies here? Then, centuries later, did King Arthur hold court here or merely camp on his way across the Moor?

What we see now is a hollow, just 65.5 feet wide and 154 feet long, with 56 stones visible, some still on the banks looking ready to fall over, some half hidden by gorse, some now flat and some carefully shaped. The ground inside the stone rectangle is low lying and wet so it has been suggested it was simply a pond, but it seems likely to have had a more interesting past. Though it's known as King Arthur's Hall it takes a fair stretch of the imagination to give it that romantic colour. Very little is known about this structure, but recent investigations by archaeologists hope to shed some light on its purpose. Excavations in 2022 revealed part of the stone structure of the banks. Pollen, peat and water samples were taken and the banks were examined using optically stimulated luminescence to reveal more about its history.

The moorland around the Hall is not as wild as it seems: grassy tracks cross from all directions, and cattle, sheep and ponies graze between the stone remains, but the Hall is fenced off from farmed livestock and this might give us a picture of how the Moor would have looked in ancient times. Stand here and imagine what life was like 6,000 years ago, but go well booted in winter – particularly because the ground on the Downs can be wet and in places boggy – and stick to the grassy tracks.

Address SX129779, www.what3words.com/hike.overpaid.flight | Getting there By car, take minor road east across Lady Down, park at side of road just before the South West Water compound and walk north across the moor for half a mile; if approaching on foot, take path west-east from Treswallock Downs to Garrow Downs | Hours Accessible 24 hours | Tip The well-known beauty spot of the medieval clapper Delford Bridge over the De Lank River is just 1.8 miles away but can get very busy on sunny days in summer.

3 Starling Roost

Startling starlings

Starlings are lovely, intelligent birds; they look black from a distance but seen close up their wings are glossy with a sheen of purples and greens. They eat spiders, moths, leatherjackets, fruit and earthworms, and are regular visitors to bird tables. But what makes them really special is how they behave at sunset in winter, just before they settle for the night: they gather together in vast numbers in the air, darkening the sky, to perform astonishing displays, seemingly a single gigantic organism with each single bird perfectly synchronised with its neighbours.

This is one of nature's winter glories. In autumn, starlings start to fly in from mainland Europe to spend the winter here and join the small resident flocks gathering together at particular sites where they can roost overnight in safety. By November, the birds are gathering from all over Cornwall towards their main roosts on the reedbeds at Marazion Marsh and the conifer plantations at Davidstow Moor. You can see these murmurations at dusk, thousands of birds dancing together in the wintry sky for 30–45 minutes before they suddenly drop down together to their roosts as darkness descends. You can see them again in the morning but you need to be there at least half an hour before sunrise.

Murmuration sites occasionally disappear and then reappear again, as the starlings decide to try another place. But the conifer plantation just below Rough Tor is one of the best places to see them, thousands of birds gathering together to roost on the fir trees; an infra-red camera will show them as bright dots against a black wooded landscape. Marazion Marsh in Mount's Bay is easier to get to and you can watch from the nearest road, but – as is always the case with wildlife – their presence cannot be guaranteed; they might have moved on to other reedbeds such as Poldhu Cove (pictured here) near Mullion. Wrap up very warm and take a torch.

Address Roughtor Road, Camelford, PL32 9QG, for Rough Tor car park | Getting there Rough Tor is signposted from the A 39 on the northern edge of Camelford | Hours The last hour before dark in November | Tip Rough Tor (pronounced 'Row Tor', as in having an angry row) is 437 yards high, with spectacular views and ancient Neolithic and Bronze Age artefacts.

4 Temple Church

The house of the Knights Templar

The Knights Templar was a famous military order established in the early 12th century to protect Christian pilgrims *en route* to the Holy Land after Jerusalem was captured from Muslim control in 1099 during the Crusades; these pilgrims were often in danger as they had to travel through Muslim lands. It is thought that pilgrims from Ireland travelled overland from Padstow down to Fowey on their way to France, avoiding the dangerous sea voyage round Land's End. The Templars were granted land in Cornwall by King Stephen and they built a hospice and chapel at Temple to provide refuge for these pilgrims. It is hard to envisage these fierce warriors, wearing their white tunics emblazoned with a red cross, here in this quiet bucolic country in the middle of Bodmin Moor.

The Templars were dissolved by the Pope in 1312. Much of their wealth was transferred to a rival order – the Knights Hospitallers – but King Edward II of England probably took as much as he could. St Catherine's Church was built here in its place. The Templars took vows of poverty and chastity and abstained from drinking and gambling. How different things were later, when the church became the Gretna Green of Cornwall, where marriages could be conducted without licences, bad marriages were consummated, and suicides (sins against the Christian faith) were buried in consecrated ground. After such marriages became illegal in 1753, the church lost its congregation and by the mid-19th century stood in ruins; a final service was held on 29 January, 1882 and it was rebuilt following the original ancient foundations by the prominent architect Silvanus Trevail in 1883.

If you visit the church today you will find a Knight on horseback and Templar emblem in the stained-glass windows. Services are held occasionally by candlelight (there is no electricity here) and there is a quiet sense of great antiquity.

Address Temple, Bodmin, PL30 4HW | **Getting there** By car, follow signs to Temple from the A30; limited parking outside the church | **Hours** Accessible 24 hours | **Tip** Take the next turning east on the A30 for Colliford Reservoir, which has picnic areas, lakeside walks with good views of bird life, and opportunities for traditional fly-fishing.

5 _ St Juliot Church
A pair of blue eyes

This is not just another church but one with a unique and romantic history: the author Thomas Hardy first met his wife Emma Lavinia Gifford, who was sister-in-law of the rector, here. Her eyes were blue - 'blue' as the autumn distance… a misty and shady blue'. As so often, when things turn out for the best, they met by chance, because the architect who should have been planning the restoration of the church had died, leaving Thomas, his assistant, to take on the task. He stayed in the Rectory and they fell in love; he walked the romantic coastal hills by her side as she rode her horse. They married four years later in 1874, after his novel *A Pair of Blue Eyes* had been serialised in a magazine. Although it had an idyllic start, the marriage was not happy – Emma never let him forget she was of a higher social class than he was – and there were no children.

In 1914, two years after Emma's death, Hardy married his young secretary, but the ghost of Emma haunted him until his own death in 1928. His heart was kept in a biscuit tin before being buried in Emma's grave in Stinsford in Dorset, with the ambiguous inscription *Here lies the heart of Thomas Hardy*, but his ashes lie in Poets' Corner in Westminster Abbey. The gossip that the doctor's cat ate the heart is perhaps apocryphal.

To commemorate the links, the Thomas Hardy Society donated the new engraved window on the sunny side of the church to mark the Millennium; on it you can see the winding path that led Hardy from his Dorset home up to the church. Depending on the light, the engraving may be best seen from outside, although the inscription will be back-to-front. In spring, one can walk through a carpet of celandines and primrose, yellow against the green. Beeny Cliff is just two miles away to the north, and Hardy's eponymous poem describes: '… the woman riding high above with bright hair flapping free, The woman whom I loved so, and who loyally loved me.'

Address Boscastle, PL35 0BT | Getting there By car, turn off the A 39 at Trewannion Gate just south of Otterham Station; drive about 2 miles to a ford over the river Valency, after which turn sharp left and drive 0.6 miles | Hours Generally open during daylight hours | Tip The fishing village of Boscastle, 3.5 miles away, suffered devastating flooding in 2004, and people had to be rescued by helicopter.

6__ Brenda Wootton
The Voice of Cornwall

At one time – in the 1970s and 1980s – many in Cornwall, Cornish and incomers alike, would have agreed that Brenda Wootton was indeed the Voice of Cornwall, in part because of her sweet soprano singing voice. Her collaborations with the Cornish songwriter Richard Gendall and her early accompanist – the father of Cornish folk music, John 'the Fish' Langford – are the stuff of folk legend, and not just in Cornwall. Brenda played her part in the revival of Cornish musical arts, and was duly created Cornish Bard in 1997, and though her generation of folk artists has mostly passed into history, the current folk scene in Cornwall has grown immensely.

Brenda's joy in singing, her energy and love of all things Cornish started her on her musical career, beginning at the Botallack Count House where you can find a blue plaque dedicated to her. She is probably best remembered for the Pipers Folk Club that she instigated at St Buryan, eventually moving to the Western Hotel in Penzance. There, down in the tiny basement every Saturday night, the audience were treated to performances by singer and guitarist songwriters that included Ralph McTell and Michael Chapman.

Brought up in West Penwith, Wootton lived and died in Cornwall, and from her rich and well-lived life she has left a strong legacy of Cornish folk singing, although sadly only a small part of her recorded work is still available to purchase; she was signed by RCA records but sadly no recordings were released. The songs of her early career have become Cornish folk scene traditionals but Brenda went from strength to strength beyond the Pipers Club, singing in English, Cornish and Breton. She developed a following in Brittany, regularly travelled to the Cornish diaspora in Australia and Canada, and even had a chart topper in Japan. Her gravestone in Paul Churchyard has a suitably Celtic theme, distinguished by an ancient Celtic triskele symbol.

BRENDA WOOTTON
1928 - 1994
Cornish poet, singer and ambassador for Cornish music and culture.

Awarded by
BBC Radio Cornwall

British Plaque Trust

Address Botallack Count House, St Just, Penzance, TR19 7QQ | Getting there Park at the car park at Botallack; bus 18 from Penzance to St Ives passes the edge of the village, from which it is just over a 0.5-mile walk to the Count House | Hours Botallack Count House accessible daily 10am – 4.30pm | Tip The annual Cornwall Folk festival, Wadebridge, is a chance to see local, national and international stars (past performers have included 3 Daft Monkeys and Seth Lakeman), with a wide cross-over element (think blues, jazz, shanty, etc); it's normally held on August Bank Holiday weekend.

7 — The Barge Tearoom
Tea afloat the only canal in Cornwall

Gently floating on the still waters of Bude Canal lies The Barge, a specially constructed wide-beamed boat made for waterside dining. You won't get seasick here as you eat your cream tea, fishcakes or egg and mayonnaise ciabatta, provided by the friendly staff. Entry is down a small gangplank and through a sliding door. Inside you can sit in the prow and look out to the sea beyond the wide expanse of Summerleaze sandy beach, or to the sand dunes beyond the river Neet as it flows to the beach, or just watch the ducks paddling past in the canal. In summer you can watch holiday makers joyfully making fools of themselves going round in circles in their hired pedalos, trying hard to turn round before they reach the end of the canal. In winter there is even a fire to sit next to.

Just beyond The Barge are the canal lock gates, one of only two working sea locks in Britain. The canal is open for boat traffic for around two miles inland from the harbour. At low tide the canal waters sits high above the sandy beach; boats can come in from the open harbour, rising up inside the lock as water pours in from the canal, so that they can shelter from winter storms. Boats go out for summer, although there are usually some yachts still present in the canal. The canal used to be 35 miles long but much has been overgrown or ploughed up; you can still see remnants of the canal in places. Canal barges were used to transport lime-rich sand to local farms but they are not needed nowadays; sand was transported from the beach by trucks along rails still visible in places on the towpath, and tipped into barges for the journey inland.

Here you can hire a rowing boat, pedalo or kayak and travel inland. If you do, keep an eye out for otters and water voles (recently re-introduced here) plopping into the canal as you pass, and look at the wooden sculptures by Daniel Sodhi-Miles recalling the canal's boating history.

Address The Barge Tearoom, The Wharf, Bude, EX23 8LG | Getting there Park in the Crescent car park, EX23 8LE, and cross the road by the canal bridge; The Barge is at the end of the towpath | Hours Daily 9am–5pm | Tip The Castle Heritage Centre, just across the towpath, houses exhibitions on military and maritime history, interactive models, Bude railway nostalgia, and information on Bude's inventive genius, Sir Goldsworthy Gurney.

8 The Battle of Stamford Hill

Roundhead or Cavalier?

The Roundheads lost this battle but won the war, and the hill is named after the losing commander! In the early 1600s, Cornwall was a Royalist county, standing firm for King Charles I against Devon and Somerset, which largely supported Parliament. On 15 May, 1643, a 5,600-strong Roundhead army of infantry, commanded by the 1st Earl of Stamford, advanced into Cornwall from Devon and took up position on this hill just north of Stratton, probably feeling invincible in this defensive position. The following day the Royalists, under Sir Ralph Hopton – hugely outnumbered with just 2,400 infantry and 500 mounted – attacked in four battalions from the south-west. After 10 hours of fierce fighting, with 300 Roundheads killed and 1,700 taken prisoner, the Royalists won the day and Cornwall was safe – for the moment – for King Charles' cause.

The battle site is now a tranquil field that is a flower-rich meadow in summer. You can stand on the hilltop and think back to 1643 and the sounds of bloody fighting and dying men. A simple sign on the roadside gate lets you know you are in the right place. In summer, pathways are mown around the field; follow any of them and you will come across a sign showing the battle stations. In May, on the closest weekend to the anniversary, there is often a re-enactment of the battle over two days by members of the Sealed Knot re-enactment society; you'll hear the beat of real drums and the crack of muskets, and smell the gunpowder. But it's doubtful they will have a 7-foot 4-inch, 32-stone giant amongst the Royalist army as they did in 1634: it is said that they had amongst their number one Anthony Payne, the Cornish Giant, a Falstaff-like local yeoman and personal retainer to Sir Bevil Grenville, the commander of one of the Royalist battalions. Payne's portrait can be seen in the Royal Cornwall Museum in Truro.

Address Between Poundfield and Poughill, near Stratton | **Getting there** From Bude drive north on the A 39 past the turn for the A 3072, and take the next turning left; drive over the hill and the entrance gate is on the right | **Hours** Unrestricted | **Tip** Sir Goldsworthy Gurney, gentleman scientist, inventor and pioneer of applying steam power, lived in Reeds, a small house on the outskirts of Poughill.

STAMFORD HILL
BATTLEFIELD SITE

SITE OF THE CIVIL WAR BATTLE OF STRATTON
16 MAY 1643

ONE OF FORTY SEVEN NATIONAL BATTLEFIELD SITES ON
ENGLISH HERITAGE'S REGISTER OF BATTLEFIELDS

THIS PLACE SITE IS OWNED AND MANAGED BY

BUDE · STRATTON
TOWN COUNCIL

WWW.BUDE-STRATTON.GOV.UK

9 Millook
Flat-packed rocks

You wouldn't think, going to this isolated site down a steep, narrow Z-bend of a road on a valley side, that you were heading for somewhere famous. If you can squeeze your car into the narrow space by the side of the road, you should head down to this cove on foot: walk past Millbrook Water, which makes a pond by the roadside, and start across a rather unwelcoming stony beach of large pebbles, rounded by endless tossing around by the North Atlantic seas. Look to your right and you will have your first view of one of Britain's top 10 geological sites, as voted for by the Geological Society of London – the cliff face.

The cliffs here on the north Cornish coast are a mix of sandstone and shale rocks; the darker shales are softer, so that these cliffs often crumble and slip down towards the sea; the harder, lighter-coloured sandstones better resist the eroding forces of the wind and sea. Here at Millook these lie in alternate layers, deposited when they were sea-bed, then forced skywards around 320 million years ago, twisted and deformed into the zig-zag folds you see before you as the earth heaved and pushed at its crust. The pattern is so complex that it is difficult to follow one of the single layers to see how it threads through the cliff, and it's easy to imagine the sheer power of the planet's geological forces, just as you would look differently at 'solid' earth if you've ever stood on ground shaking in an earthquake.

Not being the traditional sandy beach, Millook is a lovely peaceful place to picnic and gaze out to sea over the wave-cut platform of sandstone ridges and shale gullies that are exposed at low tide. Occasionally you will see surfers here – there is a left-hand point break – but it is not a suitable beach for swimming. The beach hut is available for rent (Demi Moore and Kate Winslet have stayed there) – you can't get much nearer the sea.

Address Millook, Poundstock, EX23 0DQ, www.what3words.com/spenders.dynamics.lays | Getting there By car from the A 39 at Coppathorne (signposted Bude) turn left by the pub and continue for 1.2 miles to the bottom of the valley; the cliffs are on the right | Hours Unrestricted | Tip Millook Valley Woods, owned by the Woodland Trust, cover 44 acres of a deep coastal valley, accessed by various public footpaths.

10__Dupath Well

Whoop, whoop, hurray

This lovely little holy Christian well is set in a small grassy enclosure surrounded on three sides by trees, amidst a tranquil, bucolic, rural landscape, seemingly miles from anywhere. Although small to modern eyes, it is the largest well house in Cornwall. Dating from the early 16th century, and dedicated to St Ethelred, it is made of weathered Cornish granite now patterned in grey lichen – a sign of age – and is topped by a small bell turret with weathered pinnacles at each corner.

You can open the old wooden door under the curved archway and walk into the building; let your eyes get accustomed to the sudden dark and see the overlapping granite slabs that make up the roof. At your feet is the well itself. Water runs from a spring in front of the door along a small runnel into the small granite basin built crossways at the end, and in wet weather water flows out through a pipe to the back of the building. Candles and flowers are often placed here as votive offerings.

It is said that the water here will cure whooping cough (pertussis), but it's doubtful that anyone believes this today. Baptisms were probably carried out here in the past and it is still used as an oratory, a quiet place where people can meditate and pray, sitting in the small fenced enclosure where the only sounds are those of the birds singing.

It is hard to imagine now that once, according to legend, a long, hard duel was fought here between the wealthy Gotlieb and the poor knight Sir Colan for the hand of a Saxon maiden. She preferred Sir Colan, who won, killing Gotlieb, but in remorse built the well to atone for his sins, before he also died, fatally wounded. It would have been much better just to have tossed a coin for her hand; the maiden never married anyway, and thus the battle – and both deaths – were in vain.

Address Dupath Lane, Callington, PL17 8AD, www.what3words.com/rhino.really.growl |
Getting there By car, take the A388 from Callington towards Saltash for 1.2 miles to the
sign for Dupath Well; after 550 yards turn right into the farmyard and park; walk across the
farmyard and downhill to the well | Hours Accessible during daylight hours | Tip Just one
mile west of Callington lies the Iron Age enclosure of Cadson Bury.

11 Kit Hill

Look across to England and be happy you're in Cornwall

You can't really miss Kit Hill. Its height and shape have earned it the curious title of 'a Marilyn hill' – its qualification being the drop on all sides being over 490 feet. Surprisingly there are only five Marilyns in Cornwall, the others being Brown Willy, Hensbarrow Beacon, Carnmenellis and Watchcroft. So – a good reason why this is the site for an annual Midsummer bonfire.

It is exhilarating standing at the top of this hill; the view is quite spectacular! It's fun to look at the signposting diagrams at the foot of the tower to spot the Tors, churches, downs ('downs' are 'ups' in Cornwall) in the landscape for miles around. You'll be looking east, south and west but there is no plaque for the north – is that England that you can see in the distance?

What you notice most of all is the mine stack of the Kit Hill Great Consols Mine on the highest point, although this has been rather brutally repurposed as a mast for modern technology. Love it or hate it, at least the stack still earns its keep. Kit Hill is now a country park and because this is Cornwall, yes you guessed it, the landscape is scattered with mine workings, so you need to be careful if you want to walk away from the paths.

Humans have been busy on this hill for thousands of years. There are traces of medieval surface mining, a prehistoric field system and a Bronze Age barrow under the levelled ground of the enclosure. More recently, in 1868, local landowner Sir John Call saw fit to create the earthwork enclosure next to the mine stack, with the intention of being buried there (in the end he was not), but also to commemorate the Saxon battle of Hingston Down in A.D. 838. The enclosure is a Scheduled Monument; the embankments and corner bastions are best seen from the higher ground at the mine stack. The hill was given to the people of Cornwall by the then Prince Charles to mark the birth of his son Prince William.

Address Kit Hill, Callington, PL17 8AX, www.what3words.com/prowess.nightfall.noble | Getting there By car, take the A390 from Callington towards Gunnislake for six miles; take the first left to the top of the hill, and the park is on the left | Hours Unrestricted | Tip Kit Hill affords the best view of Hingston Down, where the Cornish were defeated by the Saxons under King Egbert in 838, the last battle for Cornwall.

12 Carn Brea Castle
Dine in granite on top of the hill

It feels like a different age up on top of Carn Brea (Cornish for 'rocky hill'), 730 feet above sea level. The track up the hill is narrow, bumpy and winding, and can be busy on hot summer afternoons, when you might need to pull into the side or even reverse the car, but it is worth it for the spectacular views across Camborne and Redruth and the flat green fields to the north Atlantic coast.

At the highest point nearby is the Bassett Monument, a granite obelisk 88 feet high, dedicated to local mine owner Francis Bassett – Baron de Dunstanville – who died in 1835. The Bassetts were immortalised in Winston Graham's *Poldark* novels, a fascinating saga of family tensions and political intrigue set in an 18th-century west Cornwall mining landscape, adapted for television by the BBC. In these novels the Bassetts compete with the Viscounts of Falmouth for political supremacy.

Eastwards past the Monument, along a narrow lane past high rocky outcrops and over the brow of the hill, you reach the castle, which was built almost exactly 500 years before Francis Bassett died. The castle, once part of the Bassett empire, looks as though it had grown organically out of the rock, incorporating some Neolithic stones from an ancient building and built to match the pattern of the boulders underneath.

The castle's latest incarnation is as a restaurant, run for over 30 years by the Sawalha family, who brought a taste of Jordanian cuisine to Cornwall. In winter it is great to sit in candlelight by the fire, safe and warm inside the thick granite walls, protected from the elements, although the swirling Cornish mist and blowing rain will probably hide the glorious view. On summer evenings as you dine you can feel the lightness of being so high above the town, and late into the night you can watch the sun go down into the Atlantic ocean.

Address Carnkie, Redruth, TR16 6SL, www.carnbreacastle.co.uk | **Getting there** By car from Carnkie village, drive to the top of Carn Brea hill, and take the narrow signposted road over the hill and down to the castle | **Hours** Restaurant open daily 6–10pm; booking recommended | **Tip** The Giants, or Carn Brea Well, lies on the northern slopes below the castle, on a narrow, winding path through the bracken; it is a small well and can be hard to find.

13 National Dahlia Collection

Shall I eat it or just fall in love with its colours?

Cornwall is lucky enough to be home to the stunning collection of flowering plants that is the National Dahlia Collection, the collection of Dahlias that wins Gold Medals at the Chelsea Flower Show. Curiously, this flowering plant was found in Mexico, where it was grown as a food crop and for water piping (the stems are hollow) by the Aztecs; it has a juicy tuberous root that is still used in Oaxacan cooking. But as a food it didn't catch on in Europe: it was its natural ability to produce stunning flower colour, shape and size that impressed the Europeans. If you love rich sultry reds, the most delicate of pinks or glowing oranges you will love this place in July and August, when the plants explode into flower. For even the most discriminating gardener there will be a flower amongst the many that catch the eye.

You are free to wander along the rows of exuberant growth, admiring and photographing, and there is often someone on hand to advise how to grow them. The Royal Horticultural Society has at least 57,000 registered cultivars, and the National Collection has over 1,600 named forms and species. Beloved by Marie Antoinette, the astonishing range of colouring (all except blue) is down to its eight sets of chromosomes rather than the normal two. You may find you become addicted – there is a Cornwall Dahlia Society, which holds shows where flowers at the peak of perfection can be admired.

From its beginnings in the Duchy College, the collection moved to Longrock and then to Kehelland, where it is run as a charitable trust on a leased field at the Kehelland Trust. It's not a commercial garden centre, so don't expect to find plants for sale, though in season you will be able to buy cut dahlias and maybe some tubers, and there are sometimes volunteering opportunities.

Address Kehelland Trust, Kehelland, Camborne, TR14 0DD, www.facebook.com/
nationaldahlia | Getting there In the centre of the small hamlet of Kehelland | Hours Check
the facebook page for details | Tip Hell's Mouth (aka Porth Neigwl) is a small inaccessible
cove on the north coast enclosed by a 300-foot cliff drop. Supposedly used by smugglers,
it can be seen from a dangerous but breathtaking section of the coastal footpath, a brilliant
place to watch seabirds and crashing waves.

14   Puffing Devil
Capn Dick's puffer

At 9 o'clock on an April morning, Trevithick Day kicks off with the arrival of the Trevithick steam locomotive – the *Puffing Devil* – amidst clouds of steam and smoke, to begin the annual celebrations. Here you get the chance to see a fully operational reconstruction of the 1801 Trevithick high pressure steam (known as strong steam)-powered road locomotive being brought to life. Early in the morning a small team from the Trevithick Society get together outside the town, strike a match in the fire pit and spend the next three hours tending the fire to bring the steam chamber to the required 100 lbs per square inch pressure. Then they're off, rattling and blowing at a surprisingly smart speed along the road up to the centre of Camborne.

The engine weighs about four and a half tons when its 100-gallon water tank is full, so much lighter and more fuel efficient, but also more likely to blow up, than the engine his rival James Watt designed.

Richard Trevithick invented the first shell and tube heat exchanger, harnessing the power of high pressure steam for the first time. He also had to invent a safety valve to avoid explosions of the engine when the pressure of the steam became too high – the safety mechanism uses the melting point of lead to operate the valve. He didn't have time to invent a proper steering system so to 'drive' the *Puffing Devil* requires strong arms to control a simple tiller mechanism to direct the four wheels, avoiding slopes and potholes.

The song *Going up Camborne Hill*, sung by professional and amateur Cornish singers alike, can often be heard locally, although the language and versions vary; some verses talk of hefting coal for steam but others are more bawdy. The song celebrates the historic steam-engine ride up Camborne Hill to Beacon on Christmas Eve in 1801.

Address Basset Street, Camborne | Getting there The Tinner buses T1 and T2 between Penzance and Truro stop in Camborne | Hours The *Puffing Devil* operates annually on Trevithick Day (last Saturday in April) and at other seasonal events | Tip There is a fine statue of Trevithick outside the Passmore Edwards building at the eastern end of Bassett Street in Camborne.

15 Davidstow Moor RAF Memorial Museum

World War II Coastal Command, 970 feet up

Davidstow Moor airfield was opened in 1942, the highest airfield in Britain. It meant that the fighter pilots could avoid the sea mists that obscured the coastal RAF airfield at St Eval – but they had to cope with the hill fog that often clothes Davidstow Moor and which conceals the nearby hazards of Roughtor and Brown Willy, both over 1,300 feet high. American airmen were here first, refuelling before heading across to enemy-occupied France.

The airfield was of strategic importance as a base from which planes could patrol the Atlantic Ocean looking for U-boats and organise rescues for aircrews that had ditched in the sea – there is a photograph of airmen in a small dinghy, having survived for 11 days before rescue. There is also a map marking the sites of all the known air crashes in Cornwall, from which some of the memorabilia here were rescued.

The museum, at the airfield's edge, commemorates its activities and honours the people who gave their lives to the war effort. It is largely the work of one man, David Keast (helped by his wife Pat), who grew up near the airfield during the war. He will guide you round the museum, which feels a little like the Tardis – much bigger inside than you expect. It is full of stories and photographs (of war heroes), uniforms and equipment, from a crashed Hercules engine from a heavy armament Bristol Beaufighter warplane, and a working air raid siren, to silk scarves made from old parachutes.

There is a small chapel dedicated to the Coastal Command and a display for the 304 (Silesia) Polish Squadron, who flew sorties with anti-E-boat (E = Enemy) patrols in the North Sea and operations to control the Bay of Biscay airspace. There is also a cabinet devoted to the remarkable Air Commodore Joy Tamblin, a code breaker who later became Director of the Women's Royal Air Force.

Address Davidstow, Camelford, PL32 9YF | **Getting there** By car, take the A 39 north from Camelford, turn right onto the A 395 and follow the brown museum signs | **Hours** Daily Easter–Oct 10.30am–4pm; free entry | **Tip** St Clether Holy Well Chapel, just four miles to the east, stands alone in the countryside as a beautiful place of peace.

16 Poldice Copper Mine
Buddles and calciners

Poldice Mine lies in the parish of Gwennap, once described as the 'richest square mile anywhere on Earth' and 'the Copper Kingdom of the Old World'. If you look carefully, you can still see traces of copper in the green staining on some of the ruined walls. The mine was especially renowned for its tin, and also produced rare metals such as chalcophyllite and olivenite associated with the copper.

Now the site is derelict, with abandoned mine buildings and mine stacks. The abandoned buddles, in which the extracted ore was washed, give a shadowy indication of past labours; now the working apparatus has long gone, leaving just the shallow circular containers. The remains of arsenic calciners (which are heated to high temperatures) indicate the importance of the arsenic industry to the site in the late 19th century: arsenic was used as a pesticide (for example in thatched houses), to provide the colour green in wallpapers in Victorian houses, and later, in the First World War, to make poison gas.

Although derelict, the site has a rare beauty, as a special place of character in an historic landscape. The abandoned humps and hollows of the mine dumps are sparsely vegetated, as few plants can tolerate the metals, but rare mosses and liverworts – such as greater copperwort – grow here; if you see this plant you don't have to analyse the soil, you know it's full of copper. Much of the site is covered in heather, a purple covering in late summer when you can see the lovely silver-studded blue butterflies on the flowers.

Now Poldice is one of the 10 Areas of the Cornish Mining World Heritage Site, a Site of Special Scientific Interest, and lies on the Coast to Coast Trail across Cornwall from Devoran on the south coast to Portreath on the north coast. It is also part of the Mineral Tramways Project – you can walk, ride a horse or hire a bike to cycle through the valley.

Address Gwennap, Redruth, TR16 5QG | Getting there Park opposite Triplets Business Park, St Day, Redruth, TR16 5PZ, and follow the signs on foot | Hours Unrestricted | Tip You can hire a cycle from Bike Chain Bissoe, about 1.5 miles away, and follow the trail through the Poldice Valley.

17 — Penjerrick Garden
Darwin's brain coral

This garden, hidden on the backroads south of Falmouth, was left to the National Trust by the Fox family, along with a substantial endowment. However, the National Trust turned it down, saying the endowment was insufficient. It is now a magical place, with overgrown pathways under a wealth of huge tree ferns (some 16 feet high), bamboos, camellias, azaleas, a giant redwood, giant magnolias and the 'Penjerrick Cream' hybrid rhododendron, with flowers in April and May and attractive pink-red bark. You can collect a map at the entrance but you can still get lost in the tangle of pathways – if in doubt head upwards out of the wood. The lower part of the garden, reached by crossing a footbridge (be careful, the steps are slippery when wet), supports several ponds and a small waterfall.

Penjerrick was a summer residence for the Fox family in the early 19th century. Robert Were Fox (1789–1877), was a well-known scientist and a good friend of the famous naturalist Alexander von Humboldt, referred to by Charles Darwin as the greatest scientific traveller who ever lived. Darwin went round the world on the *Beagle*, setting off in 1831 and arriving home in Falmouth in October 1836. After nearly five years on board – and a dreadfully stormy last night – he left immediately on the mail coach for Shrewsbury. Captain Fitzroy, however, spent the night with the Fox family, hosted by Fox and his son Barclay, but according to Barclay's diary Fitzroy spent a sleepless night before heading off again.

Fitzroy left behind a brain coral, collected by Darwin, and you can still see it, part hidden under spotted laurel leaves, just next to the footbridge. Now partly covered in moss, it has a grooved surface that resembles the folds of a brain; these are the limestone outer skeletons of numerous corals that join together to create reef structures. You can buy different kinds for your marine aquarium – but this is a very special one!

Address Penjerrick House, Budock Water, Falmouth, TR11 5ED | **Getting there** By car from the A 39, follow the signs for Trebah and Glendurgan Gardens; after three miles, the sign for Penjerrick Gardens is on your left | **Hours** 1 Mar – 30 Sep Sun, Wed & Fri 1.30 – 4.30pm | **Tip** There is an entirely different garden experience at nearby National Trust-maintained Glendurgan, where a laurel maze, which was started into growth in 1833, is always a fun feature to engage with.

18 __ Royal Cornwall Polytechnic
The first polytechnic

Now known as 'The Poly', this building is home to the institution founded by Anna Maria and Caroline Fox in 1833 with the aim of promoting the useful and fine arts, to encourage industry, and to elicit the ingenuity of a local community well known for its mechanical skill – so covering many technical disciplines. Having gained royal patronage in 1835, the Polytechnic Hall was opened in 1836 to house an annual exhibition.

One of the first things achieved here was to raise money to install a Cornish Man Engine at Tresavean Mine in Lanner using the reciprocal vertical motion of two beam engines, one rising as the other falls, holding platforms on which men would stand to be taken up or down as the beams moved; eventually this went 260 fathoms down, and was a boon in taking miners back to the surface after an exhausting day's work.

Exhibitions at the Poly featured new inventions such as the electric telegraph, electric lighting, the telephone, the new art of photography in 1843, and even a demonstration of nitroglycerine in 1865. Alfred Nobel was awarded one of the Poly medals, issued as gold, silver and bronze for special exhibits and outstanding merit. The gold medal awards were re-established in 2023 in association with the University of Exeter to champion excellence in science, industry and the arts in Cornwall.

Nowadays, the Poly houses rooms to hire for exhibitions, clubs, conferences, Cafe Scientifique presentations and workshops on pottery, jewellery, art and design, but it is perhaps best known for its cinema showing Cornish and arthouse films, and international blockbusters. You can buy craft and design in the Guild shop on the ground floor. If you are a Poly member you can browse the books in the John Downing bequest at the back of the café on the first floor, where you can get a good cup of coffee and look down at people bustling along Church Street below.

Address 24 Church Street, Falmouth, TR11 3EG, www.thepoly.org | **Getting there**
On the main street in the centre of Falmouth | **Hours** Check the website for event details |
Tip The Falmouth Art Gallery (based at the Municipal Buildings, The Moor, Falmouth,
TR11 2RT, www.falmouthartgallery.com) has a large collection of artworks and the largest
contemporary collection of automata in a public museum, as well as the Henry Scott Tuke
collection of paintings, loaned by the Royal Polytechnic Society.

19__ Sea Shanty Festival

For this is my Cornwall and this is my home

Cornwall must be one of the most musical places in the British Isles, with its rich seafaring shanty history – music was important for life on board ship – the many church choirs, the brass and silver bands that were so important in village and town life, the miners' choirs, the Cornwall orchestras, the visiting musicians at Prussia Cove, the St Endellion festivals, and the choirs that got together recently as people found new energy from singing all types of music.

This is one of the festivals where the audience is welcome to sing along and give enthusiastic support for those on the stage. The Falmouth Sea Shanty Festival sang its first chorus in 2004 on the waterfront in Falmouth, where it remains to this day, and just like the rest of the global music community, lockdown couldn't prevent the singing, despite restricting it to a virtual format. Held over a weekend every June, the Falmouth Festival has an international look these days with singers from abroad, but the rousing Cornish singing is where the fun is to be found. And Falmouth is not the only shanty festival now – Mevagissey holds one in October and Port Isaac in April, so there is plenty of opportunity for get togethers.

Fisherman's Friends has become probably the best known of the groups since the film carrying its name was released, but there are many others that you will come across in an evening in a Cornish pub, singing together for the sheer joy of it. In keeping with the strong coastal community feel, the RNLI is one of the local charities that benefit from money at shanty concerts. One final word – it's a really good idea to learn the words to a couple of the favourites – maybe 'Trelawny' (written by Reverend Hawker in 1824) and 'Cornwall My Home' (written by the Cornish songwriter Harry Glasson in 1997) – so that you can sing along 'proper' at the Cornish shanty and folk festivals.

Address Events Square, Port Pendennis, Falmouth, TR11 3XA, www.falmouthseashanty.co.uk | Getting there Easy to find by the docks at the western end of Falmouth | Hours Unrestricted | Tip The National Maritime Museum is based in Events Square, and has a wide variety of changing exhibitions with a salty flavour, the national small boats collection, a café overlooking the harbour, and the Tidal Zone viewing platform below the waves, where you can see the tide rise and fall.

20 Trebah Garden
Champion trees and Nessie's Cornish relative

Where to start this account of this fascinating place? Well – start at the entrance and walk down the valley towards the Helford River along any of the footpaths in this 26-acre garden. If it's raining, shelter under the huge leaves in Gunnera Walk where the tallest man feels like a dwarf; find the pond where a sea serpent lives; climb to the Koi Pool, where enormous fish swim lazily; or visit the private beach at the garden's river edge. In late summer, Hydrangea Valley casts clouds of light blue across the green valley.

According to the Tree Register of the British Isles, which has a database of over 190,000 champion trees growing in Britain, Trebah has 8 UK champions, 10 country champions and 19 county champions; champions rank the highest with regards to tree height, spread and trunk circumference. Heights are measured with a clinometer, circumferences are measured at 4.5 feet above the ground on the uphill side of the tree, spread is measured by marking the widest and narrowest point of the crown and dividing by two.

At Trebah, the trees revel in the sub-tropical climate in this sheltered valley close to the sea and, more unusually for Cornwall, fairly safe from strong winds. The gardens lose none of their charm in winter, when many trees take on a different splendour. They include a 32-foot-high red rhododendron 'Glory of Penjerrick', a 36-foot Buddhist Yew, a 69-foot, 100-year-old Chilean Tepa, a 62-foot Japanese Maple planted in 1930, a 150-year-old 46-foot Chusan Palm, an 82-foot Hiba conifer, whose leaves release a sweet woody smell (asunaro oil) when crushed, a huge *Dicksonia* tree fern (still to be measured) and a wide 'Trebah Gem' rhododendron, bred in the garden.

There are live performances in the summer and a great café. As you leave, don't miss the newly built and planted court garden – a haven of peace.

Address Trebah Garden Trust, Mawnan Smith, near Falmouth, TR11 5JZ, www.trebahgarden.co.uk | Getting there By car, drive through Mawnan Smith towards Helford Passage and it is on your left after 550 yards | Hours Daily from 9.30am, except in extreme weather conditions | Tip Constantine Stores in the village of Constantine (Helford), just 3.7 miles away, is worth a visit for its vast array of single malt whiskies.

21 Ukraine Monument
A symbol of solidarity

The slate plaque on this simple white plinth states that it is a symbol of faith in God. The cross was erected in 1948 by Ukrainians who had escaped from Russian communism and found refuge in England.

The cross is built on the site of an old guard house at the entrance to a prisoner of war camp from the Second World War, later used to house some of the hundreds of Ukrainians who came to Cornwall, fleeing Russian oppression and wanting to practise their Eastern Orthodox Christian faith. Here, in 1947, they found religious tolerance and welcome, and jobs on the farms, in market gardens and down the mines, taking the place of the men who never came home from the Second World War. The Ukrainians built themselves a temporary chapel on this site, where they could hold services. As time went on they gradually moved out into permanent accommodation and many stayed here in Cornwall; their names still provide clues to their origins, but they are assimilated into – and active in – the Cornish way of life.

They say history never repeats itself; well it does, but never in exactly the same way. Over 70 years later, Ukrainians are again fleeing Russian aggression against their country. Ukraine gained independence from Russia in 1991 and has been a free country ever since, unlike the 1940s when Ukraine was still part of the Soviet Union and the Russians were exerting their dominance at the end of the war.

Now, as Russian armies attack the cities of Ukraine, the UK has again welcomed men, women and children with open arms, and again many of them have come to Cornwall. The memorial was re-dedicated in 2008, with many of the grandchildren of the original Ukrainian families in attendance, but with little anticipation that it would become a symbol of peace once again. It was granted Grade II-listed status in 2022 to ensure that it remains here as a symbol of British–Ukrainian co-operation.

Address On the road to Greatwood Quay, Mylor Bridge, Falmouth, TR11 5ST | Getting there By car, drive up Passage Hill in Mylor Bridge and turn right at the crossroads; the monument is at the roadside | Hours Unrestricted | Tip The 13th-century Pandora Inn at Restronguet Creek, TR11 5ST, just a mile away, is well worth a visit; you can get there by boat to avoid parking problems.

22 Bodinnick Ferry

Past Daphne du Maurier's Ferryside

Ferries are an integral part of Cornwall and from many of them you get a unique view of the river valley. The south coast is dotted with rias, those flooded river valleys that often extend far inland, meaning a long detour unless you can cross the river. The first bridge over the river Fowey is at Lostwithiel, six miles upstream from its sea mouth, so this ferry saves a lot of time, avoids a lot of traffic jams and is a green solution to a travelling dilemma. But there has been a ferry crossing between the small hamlet of Bodinnick (from the Cornish Bosdinek, meaning fortified dwelling) and the town of Fowey since at least 1344.

Throughout its earlier history, the ferry was probably a wooden deck over two hulls, rowed across the river, but in the mid-1920s it was powered by diesel – being motor driven rather than chain operated – and began to take two cars at a time. Now the ferry can take 15 vehicles but not coaches as the road on the Bodinnick side is too narrow for them. On one side you have a view over the expanse of the Fowey estuary below the towns of Polruan and Fowey, clinging to the steep valley sides: on the other you can view the beautiful wooded river valley where the trees hang down low over the water's edge.

Travelling towards Bodinnick you can see a lovely Grade II-listed white house on the right-hand side called 'Ferryside'. Dating back to the early 1800s when it was a shipwright's workshop, yard and quay, it was bought by the du Maurier family in 1926 and converted into a second home – not quite the problem for local people as we have now. Daphne du Maurier (famous for *Frenchman's Creek,* see ch. 25) lived there for part of her life, until she died in 1989. It was here that her love of Cornwall was inspired, as she looked out across the water in summer sunshine and in howling autumn south-westerly winds and lashing rain, and here that she began writing her first novel, *The Loving Spirit*.

Address Both 29 Station Road, Fowey, PL23 1DF and the Slipway, Bodinnick, PL23 1LX | Getting there By car, drive through Fowey or Bodinnick until you reach the river Fowey | Hours Frequent car ferry service daily except Christmas Day, Boxing Day and New Year's Day | Tip The Fowey Festival of Arts and Literature takes place every year; it is a tradition that 13th May, Daphne du Maurier's birthday, is always included within the dates of the festival.

23 The Tristan Stone

The travelling stone

You would not readily link this stone to the enduring but tragic love story that is played out in *Romeo and Juliet*, grand opera and a broadway musical. The stone links this part of Cornwall to the legend of the knight Tristan and the Irish princess Isolde, who fell in love when Tristan was bringing her from Ireland to marry King Mark of Cornwall. Isolde marries Mark, but the affair with Tristan continues. When Mark finds out he imprisons them both. Tristan escapes to rescue Isolde but because he is a chivalrous knight returns Isolde to Mark. Tristan dies and Isolde, arriving too late to save him, dies with him in a final embrace. Two trees – a rose and a vine – grow from their graves and intertwine their branches, never to be parted.

In Richard Wagner's opera, Tristan and Isolde drink a love potion and fall in love; the jealous knight Melot fatally wounds Tristan, who dies in Isolde's arms. King Mark pardons the lovers, but Isolde has a vision of Tristan beckoning her to the world beyond, and she dies on his body. The story is told yet again in Leonard Bernstein's *West Side Story*.

You can see this 8.5-foot stone by the side of the road out of Fowey; according to legend it marks the grave of Tristan. The stone has two inscriptions: a 'T' shape, which is believed to be an early form of Christian cross, and some faint Latin text that reads *DRUSTANS HIC LACET CUNOMORI FILIUS*, meaning 'Here lies Drustanus, the son of Cunomorus'. Cunomorus was also named Mark, king of Cornwall and Brittany. If it ever marked the grave of Tristan, it certainly doesn't now. The stone has been moved at least five times over the years. Originally it was sited near Castle Dore (King Mark's stronghold about 1.9 miles north, by the side of the B 3269), and at one time it was dumped in a ditch. You would think we live in more enlightened times, but now there is talk of moving it again for a modern housing estate!

Address Fowey, PL23 1DW, www.what3words.com/contain.broadens.zones | Getting there
By car, drive along the B 3269 towards Fowey, and the stone is on your left next to the road |
Hours Unrestricted | **Tip** The ancient coastal fort of St Catherine's Castle is a 0.6-mile walk
from Ready Money Cove along the South West Coastal Footpath; it is one of a pair of small
forts built by Henry VIII in the 1530s to defend Fowey Harbour.

24 Glow-worms at Gwithian Dunes

Green glows at night

Glow-worms shine bright green lights in the summer months. Best seen after dark in late June and July, the male beetles fly searching for females, which glow green on the grass stems and low-lying vegetation, their long abdomens curled up to display their lights. The last three segments of the female's body shine until the male lands and mates, when the light goes out as they mate to produce the next generation. All the stages glow, but the adult females are brightest, and being flightless they sit and await their mate's arrival. They will glow for three or four nights in succession and then, if no males turn up, they will run out of energy and rest there, their lights out and with no chance of attracting a mate. Late at night, if there are enough males around, all the females will have mated and there will be no sign that they were ever there; they have gone to lay their eggs in the ground and then to die.

Demelza Poldark walked out at night from her Nampara home amongst myriad glow-worms. The best way to find a glow-worm is to go out at night after 10.30pm on a clear, dry, still evening – the temperature does not seem to matter – and walk carefully across a site without using a torch (or using a dull torch) allowing your eyes to adjust to the dark. Shining a bright light on the glow-worm will probably make its light go out; without a torch you can see their tiny green glows in the vegetation at some distance – sometimes, in thicker vegetation, the light will only be visible when standing directly over the female.

One of the easiest places to see glow-worms is at Gwithian Towans, part of the coastal dune system in St Ives Bay, a popular place for walkers. But they can be found all along the coasts of Cornwall; another excellent place is Penhale Dunes, and they are even on the heathland at St Agnes Head.

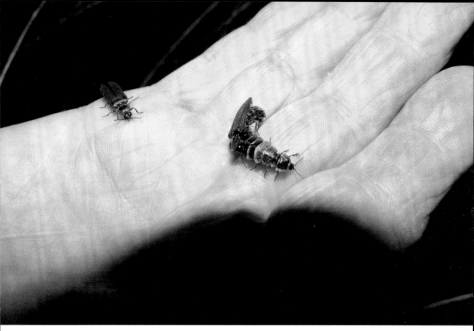

Address Gwithian Towans, near Gwithian, St Ives Bay, www.what3words.com/
joked.villa.spenders | Getting there Park at the car park immediately on the right after
turning off the main Hayle–Gwithian Road (B 3301) and walk straight across the road
into the dunes; the Atlantic Coaster route A 4 open-top bus goes from Hayle to Gwithian |
Hours 10.30pm onwards until the lights go out | Tip Get there early to see the spectacular
sunsets across the sea; if you're lucky – and have a cloudless sky – you will see the green
flash as the sun goes down.

25 Frenchman's Creek
Marriage and piracy don't mix!

This lovely secluded creek off the Helford River was made famous by Daphne du Maurier in her story of the same name. The story is set in Cornwall during the reign of Charles II, when Dona, Lady St Columb, bored with her husband in their home in London, comes down to their Cornish second home with her two children and starts a love affair with the French pirate, Jean-Benoit Aubéry. He has also escaped from the boredom of his home life in Brittany (but you must read the book to see how it ends!).

The real origin of the creek's name isn't clear and it is possible that it was named after the real life French pirate, François le Clerc, who used the creek as a base for his raids on English shipping during the Hundred Years' War. But the truth is probably more prosaic, and the creek is perhaps named after a Frenchman who lived nearby.

In fact, this is an odd place to hide a ship, as it dries out at low tide, being much higher than the main river channel, revealing deep mud banks as the water retreats. If you are not careful, your boat could get stuck here for several hours until the river waters flood back. The fallen rotting trees add an air of romantic wildness to the creek, and white little egrets can be glimpsed resting on these branches. Kingfishers may flash blue along the edges. At high tide in season, if you come by boat, you may see sea bass laying down their spawn.

You don't need to be a pirate to get here, just good walking boots. It is a steep 440-yard walk down from Kestle (and even steeper going back up) across a field and into the ancient oak woodland that clothes the valley sides, with an understorey of ferns, bluebells and the white flowers of wild garlic and wood anemone. Here you can walk along an undulating pathway parallel to the creek, through National Trust woodland, glimpsing the tranquil waters through the branches of the oak trees.

Address The nearest point is Kestle, TR12 6HU, www.what3words.com/ downcast.marathon.scope | **Getting there** By foot from Kestle Barton (Manaccan, Helston, TR12 6HU), or along the coastal footpath from Helford; or hire a boat in Helford | **Hours** Accessible on foot 24 hours; by boat at high tide | **Tip** Kestle Barton, a re-vitalised old Cornish farmhouse and grounds, has a gallery, garden and tea room (cash only), open Tue–Sun 10.30am–5pm.

26 Helford Ferry

Save your legs on the South West Coast Path

Helford Ferry is based in Helford Passage, on the north side of the river Helford. It runs just over 660 yards across the river to Helford Point, just north of Helford Village, on the other side, and from there it's a 328-yard stroll into the charming village itself. This saves you about 14 miles if you were to go all the way round by land.

Taking 12 people at a time, the ferry crosses between the Ferry-boat Inn on the north shore to the lovely thatched Shipwright's Arms on the south. Legend has it that King Canute mentioned the ferry in 1023 (although it wasn't here that he tried to hold back the tide), and it is mentioned in the Domesday book of 1086. Some of the men of the 1497 Cornish Rebellion, who gathered at St Keverne, probably used the ferry on the first leg of their journey to London, and the men, women and children on the 500th anniversary march in 1997 also crossed here.

In the 19th century the ferry was a large boat that could even carry carriages and cattle, but horses had to swim along behind, tethered to the back. It is claimed that General de Gaulle landed somewhere here in June 1940, following France's fall to German occupation, before he went to London to give his famous BBC broadcast of *L'appel du dix-huit Juin* to oppose the French-German armistice; perhaps the ferry collected him from a larger boat.

The word 'Helford' is thought to be a combination of the Cornish word *Heyl* for tidal inlet and the English word *fordh* for a crossing point. As you cross you can see the open waters of Falmouth Bay downriver, and upriver the tree-lined shores of the creeks. You can hire a boat here and row or motor up the river as far as Gweek, past the ancient oak forests, where the branches dip into the water at high tide. But check the tide and make sure that you have enough time to return before the waters recede from the high mud banks that characterise the river.

Address The Kiosk, Helford Passage, Falmouth, TR11 5LB | Getting there There are car parks on Ferry Boat Hill, Helford Passage, TR11 5LB and at Orchard Lane, Helford, TR12 6JU | Hours Daily 1 Apr–31 Oct 9.30am–5pm, depending on the tide; extended hours in summer | Tip The church of St Anthony in Meneage sits in a quiet corner just above the shore on Gillan Creek and is well worth a visit; at low tide there are stepping stones over the muddy creek.

27 __ Blue Anchor

600 years of Spingo Ale

Visit this lovely old pub and sit at the bar, or by the fire in the back-room, and order its famous own-brewed Spingo Ale, produced using water from its own well. It comes in Middle (strong), Best (strong) and Special (stronger). There's no weak version, as Spingo derives from the old English word 'stingo' or 'strong beer', so be warned. Many can attest to its particular potency. You can buy a Flora Daze beer which is a bit weaker, to give you strength to survive the famous annual Helston Flora dances on 8th May. While you are here you can try your hand in the old skittles alley with your friends, or in summer sit in the beer garden at the back.

Cornwall's oldest brewery is here at the back of the pub, although years ago it would have been in the pub itself. The first beers and mead here would have been brewed by the monks, as the pub used to be a monks' rest, from which the monks would perhaps sell beers catering to pilgrims on their way to St Michael's Mount. Water was often not safe to drink in those days, so beer was the drink of choice; come and get Spingo'd if you dare!

The name Blue Anchor is rather odd for a building high above the river Cober, which flows two miles to the sea at Loe Pool. There are theories that Helston was once a seaport but there is no evidence of this, as the shingle beach at Loe Bar blocks the entrance to the sea. There is even a painting of a sailing ship in Helston harbour. This is entirely fanciful, although it is feasible that boats could have beached at Loe Bar and have their cargo transferred to smaller boats which – in the years before the river silted up with mining waste – were then rowed up to Helston. Even then, why use an anchor on a pub halfway up a hill? It may instead be that an anchor was a Christian symbol for hope for the pilgrims, a sign that this was a place of rest and refreshment on their way to St Michael's Mount.

Address 50 Coinagehall Street, Helston, TR13 8EL, www.spingoales.com | Getting there By car, take the A 394 to the car park by the Boating Lake in Helston; walk up Monument Road as far as the Grylls Monument and turn right into Coinagehall Street; the pub is on your right | Hours Normal pub hours | Tip Feed the ducks at the Boating Lake, but be wary of the swans when they're nesting; in good weather take a turn on one of the little paddle or rowing boats.

28 Bob Fitzsimmons
The bigger they are, the harder they fall

Bob Fitzsimmons coined this famous phrase. Although he only lived in Cornwall for 11 years he is renowned as one of the county's greatest sportsmen – if not the greatest. According to his birth certificate, he was born on 26 May, 1863 and his mother's maiden name was Strongman, which was very apt, as Bob had a tremendous punch. In 1873 he left with his family for New Zealand, where he became a blacksmith after he left school. It was in New Zealand that he learned to box, and you have to go to Timaru to see his statue – he is acclaimed as one of New Zealand's greatest sportsmen. But in Helston, you can see the thatched cottage where his family lived before they left the county.

In New Zealand, Bob worked at his father's forge, where he developed strong arms and shoulders over a slim waist. He didn't look like today's fighters, being just 5 feet 9 inches tall – 11 inches shorter than Tyson Fury – and he was mocked for his red hair, abundant freckles and skinny frame. But after learning to fight in New Zealand and then Australia he went to America, where he won the World Middleweight title in 1891 by knocking out Jack Dempsey in New Orleans. In one fight, one of his referees was Wyatt Earp, Marshall of Tombstone (Bob was disqualified in this fight for a low blow).

In 1897, he won the World Heavyweight title by knocking out 'Gentleman' Jim Corbett at Carson City, Nevada in the 14th round with a left-handed punch to the solar plexus, despite Earp being in Corbett's corner. The fight was filmed and you can still see part of it on YouTube. In 1899, and again in 1902, Fitzsimmons was beaten by James J. Jeffries, who was a much bigger man. Then in 1903 Fitzsimmons beat George Gardner over 20 rounds to win the World Light-heavyweight title in San Francisco. He retired in 1914 and died of pneumonia in 1917 in Chicago, where you can find his grave.

Address 61 Wendron Street, Helston | Getting there Park at Wendron Street car park, just over 100 yards downhill from the house | Hours Viewable from the outside only | Tip The most southerly railway in Britain, Helston Railway (www.helstonrailway.co.uk) is just over 1.5 miles at Prospidnick (TR13 0RY) and runs both steam and diesel trains.

29 — Hal-an-Tow

Summer is a come, O!

The ancient festival of Helston Flora is famous around the world. The whole town stops work, the houses and shops are decorated with sycamore, bluebells and lily of the valley, and the insistent beat of the drum accompanies you everywhere – and you can't stop walking to the pace of this beat. This is a day of dances: the Early Morning Dance at 7am, the Children's Dance at 9.50am, the Evening Dance at 5pm and – most famous of all – the Midday Dance. People dance in sunshine, wind or rain (although the children's dance is occasionally cancelled for bad weather).

But the highlight for some is the Hal-an-Tow: the Town Band takes a rest here, no need for music, as the participants make as much noise as possible as they parade round the town, blowing whistles, sounding horns and shouting as they go.

It's a rowdy pageant, rehearsed several times before the day so that everyone knows the words of the chorus – *Hal-an-Tow, Jolly rumble O* ... The play is acted out at seven stations around the town, starting in the lower town, singing of Robin Hood and Little John, the Spaniards of Mousehole, St George and the Dragon, St Michael and the Devil, and Aunt Mary Moses. At the start of each playlet the Crier welcomes Cornish Cousin Jacks and Jennies, plus everyone from around the world (for it is an international festival), including the Sowsnek (Cornish for 'the English'). Then they're off. You can follow them around town, singing and shouting, or wait for them at one of the stations, then everyone crowds in behind the actors.

The Hal-an-Tow celebrates the triumph of good over evil and the coming of summer. It was abandoned in the 19th century, being considered too rowdy and disorderly, but revived in 1930 in celebration of Cornish cultural history. Anyone can join in provided they attend the rehearsals beforehand. It's great fun and the energy it generates will revive the dullest spirit.

Address Round Helston town | **Getting there** Parking is difficult on Flora Day – look for the special parking arrangements | **Hours** 8th May every year, except when the 8th falls on a Sunday or Monday, when it's danced on the previous Saturday | **Tip** The Midday Dance is the most sedate and formal, and confined to invited people and the Helston born; gentlemen wear top hats and tails, and ladies wear their finest ball gowns and fancy hats. It is a spectacular sight, even in the rain.

30 Museum of Cornish Life
Save a life for 20p

In Helston Museum there is a lovely automaton made by Carlos Zapata of Falmouth showing the life-saving apparatus invented by Henry Trengrouse. In 1807, Trengrouse witnessed the wreck of the HMS *Anson*, driven by gales onto the shingle beach of Loe Bar, with the loss of about 100 lives. The main mast collapsed and though some men gained the shore along the mast, others leaping from the ship into the sea would have been swept back without chance of escape by the backwash under their feet as the shingle collapsed back into the giant waves.

A cannon rescued from the shipwreck stands outside the Museum entrance. Shaken by the tragedy – the ship was so close to shore that witnesses could see the drowning people – Trengrouse invented his 'Rocket' lifesaving apparatus. By this method, a rocket was fired from ship to shore carrying a rope along which sailors could travel in a Bosun's Chair whilst wearing a cork buoyancy aid (a forerunner of the modern life jacket). You can see a cork jacket and other items in the museum, along with many other examples of rural Cornish life. Best of all, you can place 20p in the slot and see how the model works, to help save a life (even today, people have drowned in the sea off Loe Bar).

Trengrouse did not stop there. After seeing the bodies of the ordinary seamen buried without shrouds or headstones in the shifting sandy shingle on Loe Bar and adjacent cliffs (though Captain Lydiard, as a gentleman, was buried in Falmouth with full military honours), Trengrouse petitioned the local Member of Parliament to stop the practice of burying shipwreck victims in unconsecrated ground near the site of a wreck. Thomas Grylls, a Helston lawyer, drafted what became known as the Grylls Act, requiring that such bodies should be laid properly to rest in the nearest consecrated ground, and the Burial of Drowned Persons Act became law in 1808.

Address Market Place, Helston, TR13 8TH | Getting there Park at Wendron Street car park, just over 100 yards from the traffic lights near the Museum | Hours Mon–Sat 10am–4pm | Tip 270 yards down Coinagehall Street is the Grylls Arch, built in 1834 at the cost of £324 and dedicated to Humphry Millet Grylls, a local banker, solicitor and alderman who helped keep the nearby Wheal Vor copper mine open during the 1820 recession.

31 Trelowarren Halliggye Fogou

Down into the dark; beware of spiders

This is a walk through a bucolic landscape, along a path at the edge of a wood known as Halliggye, meaning 'place of the willow trees'. At the Fogou sign, climb the slate steps and cross the grassy enclosure to the six steps down into the dark. Let your eyes get accustomed to the dark as you pick your way down, brushing past overhanging moss and ferns between narrow walls of rock; you will need a torch to explore any further.

At the end of the first passage is a tiny rectangular entrance leading into a 'creep', which formed the original entrance (now blocked). It is too small for most people to get into – people were smaller in the Iron Age! Just before this, on the left, is a longer curved passage 16 yards long, accessible to the brave. Don't try this if you have claustrophobia or arachnophobia – on the passage roofs you might see large spiders. You can stand up in the longer passageways. If you were allowed to go in winter you would see hibernating herald moths covered in dew, but the site is closed then as rare greater horseshoe bats hibernate here, preferring the even underground temperatures inside, where they are protected from ice and frost.

This is the largest fogou (from the Cornish word 'ogo' meaning cave) in Cornwall, dating back to the Iron Age; it lies within the large Trelowarren estate and is in the care of English Heritage. There are eleven others, all in west Cornwall; three of these (at Pendeen, Boleigh and Carn Euny) are probably still in their original form. No one knows what they were used for, but they must have been important sites and would have been difficult to build by hand – there were no JCBs then! The original entrances faced north, so perhaps they were used for storage, as the sun would never lighten the dark passageways, or even used as places of refuge in those dangerous times.

Address Trelowarren Estate, Mawgan, Helston, TR12 6AF, www.what3words.com/tone.random.worms | **Getting there** By car, drive through the main gates of the Trelowarren Estate on the B 3293, turning left through gates at the main entrance after about 0.8 miles, driving through a field; after about 875 yards, turn left up a small hill and the path to the fogou is on your left at the hill top | **Hours** Open during daylight hours, Easter to the end of September | **Tip** Woodland walks within the extensive Trelowarren Estate, owned by the Vyvyan family for nearly 600 years, are open to the public in summer, with a café and restaurant available for refreshments.

32   St Levan's Stone

When a pack horse can ride through St Levan's Stone

Isolated at the end of a long narrow lane near the tip of West Penwith stands the lovely little parish church of St Levan. The Celtic Saint Selevan – St Levan – was the original patron saint of the church. He used to sit upon a large lump of granite here after fishing for chad and sea bream. Either by accident or design – who knows – he thumped the rock with his staff and it split in two, leaving a wide gap through the centre. Legend has it that he made the prophesy

'When with panniers astride, A Pack Horse can ride,

Through St Levan's Stone, The world will be done'.

Luckily the gap is still narrow enough to prevent even a single horse riding through, so we are safe for a bit longer; climate change will probably get us first.

Some people see this stone as a symbol of female fertility: a 6.5-foot-high stone cross nearby might represent male sexuality, and the site was probably used for fertility rites in ancient times. There is no sign that anyone has tried to move this large natural boulder, and it is a key and beautiful part of the churchyard. Behind the pulpit in the church, set in a granite slab, is a bronze sculpture of St Levan blessing three bream.

On Thursdays from the end of July and throughout August, cream teas are served in the church, but in winter it all looks very different. This is a wild coastline, and in a communal grave here lie 23 men who drowned in March 1905 when the triple mast iron cargo ship *Khyber* was driven ashore at Porthloe Cove 1.2 miles round the headland to the west, and exposed to the full might of the Atlantic swell; only three men survived. Down the footpath to Porthchapel Beach lies St Levan's holy well, where St Levan performed baptisms, and the associated chapel and hermitage, listed as a scheduled monument. It was claimed that drinking the water from the well would cure toothache.

Address Churchtown, St Levan, TR19 6JT, www.stlevanchurch.org.uk | **Getting there** By car, on the B 3315 take the turn signposted Porthcurno and the Minack Theatre, and drive to the very end of the road | **Hours** Daily 9am–dusk; cream teas in the church, end Jul–Aug Thu 1–5pm | **Tip** To reach St Levan by car you have to pass the famous Minack Theatre; you can visit for sightseeing or book to see one of their shows. The site is very steep with a large number of steps. If you book a performance be prepared to come even if the rain is pouring down; cancellations are rare.

33 Launceston Castle
The town's hard metaphor

Launceston – pronounced 'Lanson' by the locals (or Lawnston, but never pronouncing the 'e') – is the first and last town in Cornwall, just 1.25 miles from the ancient border with Devon. Now by-passed by the A30 dual carriageway, at one time you would have had to drive through traffic jams in the town on your holiday travels from 'upcountry', or, if you were Cornish, shouting and cheering as you passed the *Kernow A'gas Dynergh* sign to cross the river Tamar back into Kernow.

What a place to build a castle, dominating the landscape and keeping watch over all who entered this most westerly country. The castle dates back almost to the Norman Conquest, when William the Conqueror's half-brother Robert built it in the Norman 'motte and bailey' style – meaning a fort on a hill with an enclosed courtyard surrounded by a ditch. Originally made of wood, but rebuilt in stone after 1166, and referred to by the Launceston poet Charles Causley as 'the town's hard metaphor', sitting on top of the town and representing its violent past.

In 1656 George Fox, one of the founders of the Religious Society of Friends (the Quakers), was imprisoned here. You could enlist here as a soldier in the Royalist army during the Civil War, when it changed hands three times in four years, before the Parliamentarians under Thomas Fairfax finally captured it in 1646. The next occupation was probably by the United States army in the Second World War, when it was used as a military hospital; more recently the now King Charles III was officially proclaimed Duke of Cornwall here in 1973.

Nowadays you don't have to be imprisoned in the castle to visit. You can get into the grounds for free during the day, though there is a fee to get into the castle, and there is plenty of information about how the castle operated in the past, as well as lovely views over the surrounding countryside to be enjoyed.

Address Castle Lodge, Launceston, PL15 7DR | Getting there In the centre of Launceston; park opposite the castle entrance at Westgate Street car park | Hours 10am–5pm in summer | Tip The castle is no 5 on the map of 'The Causley Way: A scenic and poetic walk through his home town of Launceston' – see www.causleytrust.org for details.

34 Launceston Steam Railway

Steam up along the Kensey Valley

Launceston Steam Railway is a steam enthusiast's joy. The railway is a 2.5-mile section of the old track that ran from Launceston to Padstow via Wadebridge, bought by railway enthusiast Nigel Bowman for his restored engines and opened in 1983. The oldest of the three locomotives, *Lilian*, found a home here after retiring from Penrhyn Quarry in Wales; she is 140 years old and still going strong after restoration – all eight tons of her – blowing out clouds of steam as the pressure builds. There are two other locomotives, *Dorothea* and *Covertcoat*, and they all run on the narrow (1' 11.5") gauge (the standard mainline gauge is over twice as wide at 4' 8.5"). There are visiting locomotives, a single-cylinder-boiler steam engine (hand built this century), and assorted rolling stock, as well as a diesel railcar under construction.

As you sit in a carriage, *Lilian* will take you for 1.9 miles along the bucolic Kensey Valley, with the smell of steam in the air, passing lambs scuttling across the fields as the train goes past. Newmills Station is the only stop, and there the locomotive changes ends. From here you can walk along the river, returning to catch a later train back to Launceston, to the café and museum with its vintage vehicles, old railway equipment and memorabilia from the old North Cornwall Railway.

The original North Cornwall Railway was opened in 1899 with standard gauge and a maximum speed of 55mph. It ran from sea level at Padstow up to over 650 feet, so it was a slow journey, slower in the up direction (on the railways 'up' always refers to going towards London) than the down (to Padstow) because of the climb to Launceston. The Launceston to Wadebridge section closed in 1966; the Wadebridge to Padstow section is now part of the Camel Trail, so there is now no chance of re-instating that section. However, there are hopes that more of the Launceston line might be opened to the west.

Address St Thomas Road, Launceston, PL15 8DA, www.launcestonsr.co.uk | Getting there By car, drive north through Launceston on the A 388, past the Castle, down the hill and turn right into the Newport Industrial Estate; follow the road round to the car park on your right | Hours Check the website for current information | Tip There is a holiday cottage for rent at the station itself – what could be better for a steam enthusiast?

35 Zig Zag
As I went down Zig Zag

Come zig-zagging with Charles Causley, the Cornish poet. The Zig Zag is the setting for one of Causley's entertaining children's poems:

'As I went down Zig Zag, the clock striking two,

I watched a man walk with one boot and one shoe…'

The 410-foot path, dating back to the 14th century, snakes up a rocky cliff from Station Road at the base up to Dockacre Road in Launceston. Though it used to be very busy, with over 200 people using it in a single day, it's now used purely as a short cut to and from Launceston railway.

In former days you could get a good view over the lower town down to the river Kensey, but now the trees and shrubs have grown up and obscure the view, making the walk cool on a hot summer's day. In 1912, two men digging a trench were engulfed by a land-slip up to their hips; thankfully they were dug out alive, if bruised, after two hours. Now it is tarmacked and safe, with railings, but pretty steep. Watch out for kids cycling down, zooming round corners. Catch your breath halfway up and at the top; walking down is easier!

Charles Causley spent most of his life in Launceston and died there in 2003 aged 86. He hosted the BBC's *Poetry Please* for many years, and his poems are well known; he delighted in writing for children, saying that 'there are no good poems for children that are only for children' such as 'Colonel Fazackerley Butterworth-Toast, Bought an old castle complete with a ghost …' – good for children and great for grown-ups. The Causley Trust bought his former home in 2007 and they have mapped The Causley Way, 'a scenic and poetic walk around Launceston', available on the Trust's website, and comprising 10 poems associated with 10 places in Launceston (including Zig Zag and the castle). The Trust also runs the Causley Festival at midsummer every year.

Address The starting point is at Station Court, Launceston, PL15 8EG | **Getting there** The entrance to Zig Zag is on the right behind railings at the end of Station Road, just past the railway station car park | **Hours** Accessible 24 hours | **Tip** Causley's house at Cyprus Well is on Ridgegrove Hill, and his grave is in St Thomas' churchyard in Launceston.

36 Darley Oak
One thousand years old

Dating to before the time of William the Conqueror, this is the oldest tree in Cornwall. This venerable tree is a pedunculate oak, *Quercus robur* (also known as 'English' or 'common oak', but neither name seems appropriate given its age and location!); it is mentioned in documents dated 1030, and though it looks big now, it was once much bigger: it lost half its size during the great storm of 1987, but in 1927 its circumference was 27 feet, measured from 5 feet up; the hole inside, where the heart wood had gone, was large enough for tea parties. You can imagine ladies in their silk finery and gentlemen in top hats squeezing into the hollow and sipping tea below the deadwood beetles, woodlice and spiders that would scuttle across the wood and occasionally drop onto their fancy cakes.

The Darley Oak easily qualifies as an Ancient Tree having long passed the 400-year old mark, so it was selected as one of the 50 Great British Trees by the Tree Council in celebration of Queen Elizabeth II's Golden Jubilee in 2002. It is still well leaved for such an old tree, although many branches are now leafless, and it still produces acorns. It could survive for many hundreds of years yet, though by then it might have to be propped up, so please respect this wondrous tree and admire it from outside the wall.

Why has it survived so long in this part of the country with the fewest trees? The land on which it stands was owned by the same family who cared for it for hundreds of years, and the heights of Bodmin Moor provide shelter from the worst westerly storms. Sharp Tor to the west stands 748 feet higher than the Darley Oak. Other ancient and veteran trees can be found in south-east Cornwall, in the large woodland parks of Ethy, Lanhydrock and Boconnoc, where the soils are deep and less acid, the climate is milder and the influence of the Atlantic Ocean less keenly felt.

Address Darley Farm, Liskeard, PL14 5AS, www.what3words.com/compiled.blocks.habits |
Getting there By car, take the B 3254 from Liskeard to Darleyford, then take the first left to
Darley Farm; bus 236 (Liskeard to Launceston) passes the farm entrance | Hours Accessible
24 hours | Tip Caradon Hill is just under three miles away, and you can drive to the top by
the television station mast for a glorious view across to Devon.

37 King Doniert's Stone
The last king of Cornwall

Two ancient granite stones stand in a small semi-circular enclosure on a windswept hill by the road to Minions. This site has one of the few pieces of evidence from the time called the 'Age of Saints', a time of Arthurian legend, Celtic Christianity and the kingdom of Cornovii, which became Cornwall. The only sign of the modern world here is a useful information board and the adjacent road – no gift shops or ice cream vans – but it is worth the three-mile detour from the main A38 road from Bodmin to Liskeard.

Doniert is probably the Latin name for Dungarth; King Dungarth was the last king of Dumnonia when it had been reduced to what is now Cornwall, after the Saxons had conquered the rest of the south-western kingdom. Why the Saxons stopped at the Cornish border is not known (maybe the weather was just too much for them?).

Dungarth is thought to have had an untimely death in the year A.D. 875, drowned in the river Fowey, perhaps at Golitha Falls just a mile to the west. The smaller of the two stones you see is said to mark where he was buried. Both stones are broken but carry Celtic knot patterns and it's likely that crosses – possibly wood – fitted into the holes on the top, marking this place as a Christian site. You can just make out the Latin inscription on the smaller stone: *Doniert Rogavit Pro Anima* meaning 'Doniert requested this for his soul'.

The truth is lost in the mists of time, but run your hands over the symbols and patterns that skilled men worked into the hard granite surface and imagine the ancient Cornish burying their king here near the top of the small rise over 1,100 years ago. Slow-growing lichens that cover the stones probably began their life during that ceremony.

If you are looking for refreshments, Wetherspoon celebrates this Celtic history by naming their pub in Liskeard, just six miles away, after King Doniert.

Address St Cleer, PL14 6EG, www.what3words.com/slid.unlocking.stuffy | Getting there By car, take the B 3360 to Golitha Falls, and the stones are on the right as you drive north | Hours Accessible 24 hours | Tip Golitha Falls is just over 0.5 miles away to the west; from the car park, follow the signpost for 0.5 miles.

38 Minions

Not those Minions

Real life Minions; it's a small village set high on Bodmin Moor. The earliest records of the village date to 1613, and the name is probably derived from the Cornish Menyon meaning stones. But as we know, there is also a species of very naughty creatures known as Minions who have been around since the dawn of time (according to their creators). Which came first, the village or the little yellow beings? You can argue over that, but more people know about the antics of Kevin and his chaotic crew from the various films they feature in than have heard of the village! Villagers were naturally delighted with the increase in visitors resulting from the *Despicable Me* film franchise, and proudly displayed a new road-safety sign showing three of their kind – sadly now removed.

Seriously though, Minions is a great place to visit if you are interested in Cornwall's history. It sits just a few hundred yards away from the Hurlers – the name given to granite stones placed in three circles in the Bronze Age (about 1,500 B.C.), near to which is the Rillaton Barrow, a large underground burial chamber discovered by some miners in 1837. You can see a copy of the gold Rillaton Cup, which was found in the Barrow along with human remains and artefacts, in the Royal Cornwall Museum, the original now being kept in the British Museum.

Also to be found at Minions is the Houseman's Engine House, where there is an exhibition showing the history of the area. And sitting above all this is the strange and distinctive, but almost certainly natural, rock feature known as the Cheesewring, with the remains of a railway used when the area was a busy industrial site.

The village boasted the highest pub/hotel in Cornwall till it burnt down recently, hopefully to be rebuilt soon. For those in need of refreshment after exploring there is the tearoom/post office where you will find some Minion-shaped souvenirs and a licensed café.

Address Minions, Liskeard, PL14 5LE, www.what3words.com/tangling.tribe.number | Getting there Easily found near the top of Bodmin Moor | Hours Unrestricted | Tip The Cheesewring sits above a water-filled quarry known locally as Gold Diggings quarry; there is a public right of way, but swimming is dangerous and strictly forbidden.

39___Stuart House
King Charles slept here

King Charles I stayed here for a few days in early August 1644 during the English Civil War, safe in the knowledge that there was a secret underground tunnel that he could escape through at the first hint of danger. Now locked, unsafe to use and blocked by a roof fall, it is reputed to run from here to the holy well on Well Lane just over 300 feet away.

This was the house of the Royalist, mayor and chief steward of Liskeard, Joseph Jane. Cornwall was mainly a Royalist country then, and Charles won the battle of Lostwithiel in late August/early September, the worst defeat suffered by a Parliamentarian army during the war. The Roundhead general the Earl of Essex fled across the sea, and in February 1645 Oliver Cromwell and Sir Thomas Fairfax created their New Model Army, which won the war for Parliament. Four years later, on 30 January, 1649, King Charles was tried for treason and publicly beheaded. Joseph Jane fled abroad, where he died in 1658 aged 63. His son William, born here in 1645, later played a part in the Glorious Revolution of 1688, when King James II was deposed, and William and Mary took the throne.

This is a lovely old Grade II-listed house, dating from the 15th century. It was continuously occupied until the Stuart House Trust purchased it in 1988, in order to safeguard it as an Arts and Heritage Centre for exhibitions, concerts and meetings. It has fine granite fireplaces, exposed timbers, granite mullioned windows, slate floors and a main entrance door dating from the 15th century. Climb the 18th-century staircase into the upper rooms to see the exhibitions there (including a permanent civil war exhibition) or have lunch in the tiny café at the back. On fine sunny days you can take your tea out into the lovely enclosed ornamental courtyard garden and sit at one of the picnic tables, away from all the noise and bustle of Barras Street.

Address Barras Street, Liskeard, PL14 6AB | **Getting there** Easily found on the main road in the centre of Liskeard | **Hours** Mon – Fri 9.30am – 3.30pm, Sat 9.30am – 12.30pm | **Tip** The 14th-century Pipe Well at 23a Well Lane, PL14 3TP, has never been known to run dry, being fed by four springs, and is housed beneath a small arch.

40 Goonhilly Earth Station
Who's there?

Standing stark against the everchanging Cornish sky, the 'Goonhilly dishes' have become a feature of the Lizard landscape that are just as iconic as the beautiful Lizard Point and Kynance Cove. In 1962, Cornwall was proud to be home to the first British ground station that provided the link with the European Telstar communications satellite, and there was great excitement at the creation of the station; the local taxi firm is still called Telstar taxis!

The site was ideal: sea on all sides provided minimal radio interference, and at the time Lizard was a relatively quiet corner of Cornwall. Antenna 1 (Arthur to his friends and now a Grade II-listed structure) was the first parabolic dish antenna that would be used for satellite, rather than intercontinental, communications to relay via Telstar. The site was then the largest satellite station in the world but Goonhilly was sidelined by its owners BT in 2006, the Telstar satellites were replaced and became so much space debris, and after a spell as a visitor attraction, Goonhilly was heading for closure.

Under new management by Goonhilly Earth Management Ltd, the site has risen phoenix like to become an important operational link for international space exploration, and Goonhilly provides part of the network of European Space Agency communications antennae. The site has sprouted more dishes, now all named after characters in the Arthurian legend; the largest, known as Merlin, is 105 feet across (Arthur is 85 feet across), giving the station the capability to provide communications for deep space and lunar missions including the 2022 NASA Artemis moon mission and, in 2024, the first commercial moon landing by the Intuitive Machines Odysseus spacecraft.

Nowadays the station is only open to the public on special occasions, so look out for open days linked with science festivals. Otherwise, you can see the big dish easily from viewing areas at the front entrance or further along the nearby road.

Address Goonhilly Downs, Helston, TR12 6LQ, www.goonhilly.org | Getting there Easily visible from the B 3293 | Hours Unrestricted viewing outside | Tip The underlying rock of the Lizard peninsula is a piece of oceanic crust shoved up into the continental crust by deeper forces, and the associated heathland is very special, so the whole area is a geological and biological conservation area.

41 Lizard Lighthouse
Pharology – the study of lighthouses

Lighthouses are fascinating. The Lizard could claim to have the oldest lighthouse in Cornwall but the first attempt in 1619, a private philanthropic effort, failed from lack of funding. The replacement, built in 1752, is the second oldest working lighthouse in the UK; it stands near the most southerly point of the Lizard Peninsula, the flashing beacon being an important coastal mark for ships approaching the English Channel and warning of the treacherous rocky reef that extends south beneath the waves.

There is no standard lighthouse design and some, like Wolf Rock off Land's End, are amazing feats of engineering. Four towers had originally been intended at Lizard but only two were built. The lights were originally coal fired braziers, later huge electric bulbs. The light on the western tower was withdrawn in 1903 but the eastern light continues, showing one white flash every three seconds, this being the code to distinguish its position. The beam reaches 26 miles into the channel and there is a foghorn, once the last compressed air belch in the UK from two trumpets on the cliffs operating until 1998, but now an electronic one every 30 seconds.

Just as amazing were the lives of the keepers whose job it was to keep the warning systems working in the very worst of weathers. For optimum efficiency, the beacon requires regular servicing, and those panes of glass naturally have to be kept sparkling clean. Lizard would have been a relatively easy job compared to the ones built on rocks out at sea, as it is too high above sea-level to be in danger from the waves – if the sea reaches here we are all in trouble!

Run by Trinity House – the national institution responsible for the lighthouse network, founded by Henry V in 1514 – Lizard is the only lighthouse in Cornwall that has a newly restored (temporarily closed in 2023) visitor centre where you sometimes get the chance to climb the lighthouse.

Address 3 Lighthouse Road, Lizard, Helston, TR12 7NT, www.trinityhouse.co.uk | Getting there Park at the National Trust car park near the end of Lizard Point | Hours Currently closed awaiting full restoration; check website for re-opening | Tip The old lighthouse keeper's cottages between the two towers are now self-catering cottages, but be warned, you will hear the fog horn, continually, when the weather closes in!

42 Serpentine
Not the lake in London

If you say serpentine to someone in Cornwall they think of a colourful rock – found in Cornwall, only on the Lizard peninsula – not the lake in London. The name comes from the rock's greenish colour and smooth or scaly appearance.

This intriguing rock was formed around 400 million years ago under water; contact with the water (hydrothermal metamorphism) created serpentine rock that in some places changed to red due to great compressional forces. You can see outcrops of the rock in several places on the Lizard but most famously at Kynance Cove, where the waves splash onto the cliff face above the rocky beach, bringing out the beautiful red and green markings that are barely noticeable on dry stone.

Serpentine is soft and easy to carve; it scores between 2.5 and 3.5 on the Mohs hardness scale, whereas diamond scores 10. Its use for ornamental building was popularised by Queen Victoria and Prince Albert after a visit to Cornwall and in the Great Exhibition of 1851, and they used it in Osborne House on the Isle of Wight. As nowadays, where the Royal Family led, many people followed: serpentine factories were established to meet orders, along with several small workshops, but the industry declined as the century wore on and fashions changed. There are still a few places in Lizard town where you can buy ornaments such as ashtrays (not so popular nowadays) and lighthouses.

However, serpentinite has other uses: it contains abundant hydrogen atoms, which can help shield nuclear plants from escaping neutrons, and it was used at Chernobyl. Hydrogen from serpentinization is also a potential fuel for life on other worlds; serpentine occurs on Mars and may be the source of Titan's hydrocarbon-rich atmosphere. Soils on serpentine bedrock are base rich, unlike most of Cornwall, and often very thin; they are low in calcium but high in magnesium, creating ideal conditions for many rare plants.

Address Lizard, TR12 7NX | **Getting there** Easily found at the end of the A 3083 | **Hours** Lizard shops are generally open in normal shop hours; check websites for details | **Tip** Kynance Cove, TR12 7PJ, is owned by the National Trust and is famous for its serpentine rocks, rare plants, spectacular scenery and rock stacks.

43 Britain's Most Southerly Café

Who's watching who?

The Polpeor Café offers glorious views westward over the cliffs and sea towards the sunset. This is the southernmost point in Britain (don't say England, as the locals would not like it – to them, Cornwall is a separate country). From here, you can look down at seals hauled out resting on the rocks or swimming in Polpeor Cove, their heads bobbing in the water, watching you watching them, diving down into the waves if you get too close. These are grey seals, commoner here than common seals, which have a shorter snout with nostrils close together.

If you are lucky you can see the Cornish choughs, the traditional emblem of Cornwall, with glossy black wings, bright red legs and red beaks, swooping and gliding over the steep cliffs clothed in thrift and Hottentot fig. Choughs had died out in Cornwall in 1973, the last survivor living alone on the cliffs near Newquay since its mate had died in 1967. However, they have returned under their own steam so that efforts to re-introduce them proved unnecessary. In Cornish its name is 'Palores', meaning 'digger', as it pokes its long beak into the bare ground looking for tiny things to eat.

Despite its disappearance, the chough remained on the Cornish coat of arms, standing contentedly on top of the crest, flanked by a tin miner and fisherman representing the proud traditions of Cornwall. It is said that when King Arthur died his soul left his body in the form of a chough, its red feet and bill signifying his bloody end.

So you can sit in comfort on the terrace of the Polpeor Café, under the parasols in sunny weather or inside in stormy weather, with your cream tea or crab salad or even a Kynance Burger (named after the famous nearby beauty spot of Kynance Cove). Don't forget your binoculars, as without them you will miss the wildlife that makes this place such an exciting destination.

Address Lizard Point, Lizard, Helston, TR12 7NU | Getting there Park in the National Trust car park by the lighthouse | Hours Seasonal, but generally daily 10am–5pm | Tip Along the coast lies Mullion, worth a visit for its medieval centre and St Mellanus church, where sheepdogs came and went through the Dog Door, and the carvings on the oak pew-ends date back to the 16th century.

44 Giant's Hedge
The Devil's work?

The Giant's Hedge dates back to before the Romans arrived in Britain. It is one of the largest ancient earth banks in the UK, 10 miles long, a hedge built of earth and stone, 10 to 16 feet high in places, topped by trees and flanked in places by pathways or ditches where the tread of feet over hundreds of years has created a deep lane between two high banks.

Over the years, sections of the hedge have been lost to development such as roads and farming, and in some places the bank has been incorporated into the boundary of modern fields, but you can recognise it by its height and sturdy depth. Seven sections are still easily visible in the rural landscape, and you can follow it up and down the valleys and where it crosses the narrow roads in this peaceful wooded landscape between Lerryn in the west and Looe in the east.

The structure probably dates back to the Iron Age, over 2,000 years ago, although some sources indicate that it was constructed after the Romans arrived, perhaps as a defence against the Saxons. At that time Cornwall would have been a patchwork of local settlements organised into small tribal units, with no hierarchical system with a king or queen at its head. The hedge cuts off the south-west corner of the land between the Looe and Fowey rivers, and is protected by the rivers on two sides and the ocean to the south. It would have been built to claim ownership to the south and prevent marauders from the north stealing the men's wives and raiding their livestock.

A local rhyme goes: 'One day, the Devil having nothing to do, Built a great hedge from Lerryn to Looe', thereby creating a legend to explain why such a large hedge, which had been a very real defence, would be built across such a sparsely populated countryside. There is another similar earthwork across the narrowest part of West Penwith between Lelant and Long Rock isthmus, also probably a tribal boundary.

Address Visible in several places between Lerryn and Looe | Getting there The best
remains are near Lerryn, and along a bridleway just north of Lanreath; access is easiest
at Kilminorth Woods, by the large riverside car park at West Looe, PL13 2AF | Hours
Unrestricted | Tip Looe Island is a marine nature reserve run by the Cornwall Wildlife Trust
(www.cornwallwildlifetrust.org.uk) and worth a visit by organised boat trip from Looe.

45 Lerryn Stepping Stones
Mind your step

Twenty-four hexagonal stepping stones cross the Lerryn river near the top of the tide's reach, and who can resist stepping across! Each is wide enough for the largest foot, well spaced and stable. But wait your turn – there is no room to pass another person in the middle. Be careful you don't fall in, although there is little mud at this point. At high tide, the stones are covered by water, so if you want to cross the river then, use the medieval bridge just upstream instead: it dates from at least the 16th century, and includes little triangular safe places where, in ancient times, people could step back from packhorses.

Kingfishers occasionally flash blue over the water and you can watch for little egrets slowly stalking heron-like along the river. But be aware that the little car park can flood at high tide: check your tide tables if you want to visit the pub, otherwise it is not only your sorrows that you will drown. If you come by boat from Fowey, 3.5 miles downstream, make sure that you get the tides right, otherwise you'll be stuck there in the squelchy mud until the tide comes in again – not so bad if you are in a flat-bottomed boat, though.

Lerryn looks a peaceful, tranquil village but there used to be races and rugby in the mud flats below the stepping stones; you can still buy a jigaw puzzle featuring a photo of mud rugby taken here in 1993. Now there is an annual fancy dress Seagull race, racing any kind of boat providing it is propelled by a Seagull outboard engine.

In the past, in spring, Lerryn boys and girls used to capture the maypoles from Lanreath and other local villages, and erect their own on the green on the north side of the river, taking turns in guarding it from recapture over night. It's a pity that this old tradition has now been abandoned. Now you can picnic in peace on the tables on the green or visit the Ship Inn or the lovely little shop where you can buy a nice cup of coffee.

Address Lerryn, Lostwithiel, PL22 0PT, www.what3words.com/
workbook.rehearsal.exploring | Getting there By car, on the A390 west from Lostwithiel to
Lerryn | Hours Unrestricted | Tip The lost and abandoned Tivoli Gardens can be found on
the south side of the river by walking along the road to the end of the village and taking the
footpath up through the woods; they can be hard to find!

46 The Old Duchy Palace
Should tin miners pay tax?

The Old Duchy Palace was built in 1292 by the Earls of Cornwall. The building that remains was part of a much larger complex, said to be the oldest building in Cornwall apart from castles and churches. The Duchy of Cornwall was established by Edward III in 1337, and under his son Edward the Black Prince the palace became the administrative centre for the Duchy, which now owns and manages over 128,000 acres across south-west Britain, including substantial areas of Cornwall. The Duke of Cornwall is traditionally the eldest son of the monarch and thus heir to the throne; when the monarch dies the current Duke becomes King and his eldest son becomes the Duke. Although the Duchy's administrative headquarters are no longer in the palace, the Duchy has some of its offices below Restormel Castle.

Lostwithiel has a very rich history. It was once the capital of Cornwall and was home to the Stannary Parliament, Stannary Court, a Coinage Hall and an Exchequer Hall, where money was collected. The Stannary Parliament, which represented tin miners, was recognised by King John in 1201 and exempted tinners from common taxes. The Lord Warden of the Stannaries could arrest and judge the tinners if they broke the law (though tinners had the right to search for tin on anyone's land).

In 1644, during the siege of Lostwithiel in the Civil War, the Parliamentarian army set fire to the Great Hall; the Duchy Palace survived the fire and became the place where the Stannary Parliament met until 1753. In 1988, Cornishman Fred Trull, who lived in nearby Lerryn, tried to revive the Stannary Parliament: he encouraged people to buy tin mining shares so that they could claim that the hated poll tax (a version of council tax) did not apply to them, since they were exempt under ancient Stannary law. Hundreds of people bought shares, but this daring venture failed, to the great chagrin of the Cornish people.

Address 1 Quay Street, Lostwithiel, PL22 0BS | Getting there There is free parking in the main car park next to the Community Centre | Hours Viewable from the outside only | Tip Lostwithiel Museum at 16 Fore Street (open Apr–Oct) is worth a visit, with lots of local exhibits and photographs; admission is free.

47 Mên Scryfa
Ancient stone with writing

This impressive but mysterious stone stands 5.5 feet high, solitary in a grassy meadow, inscribed in Latin *Rialobrani Cunovali fili* ('Rialobranus son of Cunovalus'). But it might pre-date the Roman occupation: is it perhaps a prehistoric standing stone which was then inscribed sometime between the 5th and 7th centuries to celebrate a local tribal leader or Cornish king? Does it mark the boundary of his land, or the place where he died?

We know little of that time. Rialobranus may have been a Christian king holding land in the Dark Ages after the Romans had left Britain. 'Rialo' means 'kingly', and his father Cunovalus may have been a famous leader and perhaps kin to King Arthur; Rialobranus may have been King Arthur's cousin. Legend has it that the stone is the height of the mighty warrior Rialobranus. Perhaps he occupied the 2,500-year-old Cun Castle, standing 700 feet high, 1.5 miles to the south-west.

We do know that, like many standing stones, it had been pushed down in later years and might have been moved from its original site. Perhaps there was a story that it was a burial site and contained treasure. In a quarry just 1.2 miles to the west, a hoard of Bronze Age gold bracelets, some from Ireland, was discovered in 1884 – but there is no evidence that there is any more treasure to be found.

The stone was resurrected in 1824 by Captain Giddy of the Royal Navy, who also rebuilt the nearby Lanyon Quoit (although not exactly as it was before). Approximately four feet of the stone is now hidden in the ground so that the last part of the inscription (*fili*) cannot be clearly seen, though it would have been visible at some time. And some 200 years later, vandals have attacked the stone leaving the top, once covered in a forest of bushy lichen, darkened by charring and covered in oil; did they also try to topple it, looking for treasure? There is no treasure – only the treasure of ancient inscriptions and mysteries that link us to our past.

Address Madron, Penzance, TR20 8NX, www.what3words.com/bronzer.applauded.mows |
Getting there By car, follow signs for the Mên-an-Tol from the road between Madron and
Morvah; then walk up the lane for 328 yards beyond the Mên-an-Tol, and the Mên Scryfa
is visible in a field on the left | Hours Unrestricted | Tip You pass the prehistoric Mên-an-
Tol standing stones on the way to the Scryfa stone. It was thought that crawling through
the hole in the stone would cure various physical ailments, including rickets, back pain and
tuberculosis, and enable a woman to realise her dream of becoming pregnant.

48 Hawker's Hut
The original man cave

The Reverend Robert Stephen Hawker was the somewhat eccentric Vicar of Morwenstow, as well as being a thoroughly good human. He was a well-known poet, he kept Robin the stag and Gyp the pig as pets, and he was a humanitarian who looked out for the ships wrecked on the rocky coast: he recovered the bodies of drowned sailors to give them a Christian burial and managed to rescue one alive from the wreck of the *Caledonian*.

The words of *The Song of the Western Men*, better known as *Trelawny*, were written by the man known to his parishioners as Parson Hawker and set to music by L. T. Clare. Its subject is Sir Jonathan Trelawny, Cornishman and bishop, who was imprisoned in 1688 by King James II because he objected to Catholics being allowed freedom to worship in Protestant England. The song has become the rousing anthem of Cornwall: 'And shall Trelawny live? And shall Trelawny die? Here's twenty thousand Cornish men Will know the reason why!'. It's sung whenever the Cornish gather together – be it at rugby matches, Fisherman's Friends performances or, best of all, 'down the pub' with your own friends. Better learn the words!

But most intriguingly, in 1834, high on the sea cliff just a mile from his church at Morwenstow, Parson Hawker built a small hut from timbers salvaged from the wrecks of the *Caledonian*, the *Alonzo* and the *Phoenix*. Here he would sit, smoking opium, writing poetry and looking out to the sea. The writers Charles Kingsley (author of *The Water-Babies*) and Alfred Tennyson (author of *Idylls of the King: The Passing of Arthur*) were entertained where you can now sit on a timber bench under the turf-covered roof. On still, sunny days you can contemplate the calm blue sea and perhaps compose a poem; on stormy days, with the lower door closed, you can scan the horizon for ships. Don't miss the steps down through the blackthorn scrub – Hawker didn't mean to be easily found!

Address Morwenstow, Bude, EX23 9SR, www.what3words.com/palms.eggplants.harvest | Getting there From Morwenstow Church, park at the tea-rooms, and keeping the church on your right take the path to the coast, turning left when you get there; the steps down are in the second field | Hours Accessible 24 hours | Tip The Rectory Farm Tearooms are worth a visit, and a path from there goes south to the Tidna Valley, where there are plans to re-introduce the iconic large blue butterfly.

49 — The Marconi Memorial
dit dit dit

Standing on this breathtaking clifftop your first thought wouldn't necessarily be of the ground-breaking early wireless development made here and commemorated by the memorial. Guglielmo Marconi began his experiments at home in Italy then came to England at the age of 22 to patent and develop his invention with a team of expert engineers. Wireless transmitting at a short distance had been successful but it was widely held that long distance transmission couldn't work because of the curvature of the globe.

Marconi thought otherwise. The selection of Poldhu clifftop for transmitter construction didn't come without problems; the Cornish weather had damaged the aerials earlier in the year, but by the end of 1901 the experiment was ready. On 12 December, Marconi sat on a hilltop in Canada holding an earphone, hoping to hear the first ever transatlantic radio signal. Using Morse code, a series of S's was to be sent from Poldhu Wireless Station to his simple receiver raised 150 feet in the air by a kite. At 12.30pm came a faint *dit dit dit*; Marconi knew the signal had come 1,700 miles from Cornwall and that wireless messages could indeed be sent round the globe.

And so began the explosion of technology that gave us broadband, mobile phones, television broadcasting and the internet. Commercial equipment quickly followed and it was thanks to the wireless radio system that in 1912 the crippled *Titanic* was able to signal for help and that 700 souls were saved. The transatlantic transmission instantly made Marconi world famous and ensured the success of his British business, Marconi's Wireless Telegraph and Signal Company. At the top of the memorial you see a globe framed by two triangles representing wide radio beams. The remains of the wireless station are still visible and an amateur radio club operates from the nearby Marconi Centre.

Address Mullion, Helston, TR12 7JB, www.marconi-centre-poldhu.org.uk | Getting there On the south side of Poldhu Cove, take the narrow road up to the care home and follow the signs | Hours Memorial unrestricted; check website for Marconi Centre seasonal opening hours | Tip The nearby Mullion Cove harbour is well worth a visit – see the webcam www.camsecure.co.uk/mullion-harbour-webcam.html.

50 Laurence Binyon
At the going down of the sun

Take a walk along the South West Coast Path round Pentire Head, looking north-west across the sea as the sun goes down, and think of those wars raging today in Europe, and the Great War of 1914 to 1918: 'At the going down of the sun and in the morning, We will remember them'. The classic poem 'For the Fallen' was written by Laurence Binyon, sitting here on the cliff top where the fourth stanza is engraved in granite. He wrote it in September 1914, just one month after the outbreak of the First World War, after the British Expeditionary Force had suffered casualties at the Battles of Mons, Le Cateau and Marne.

At 45, Binyon was too old to be a soldier, but in 1915 he volunteered as a hospital orderly in France and afterwards worked for the Red Cross in England, helping to take care of the wounded of the Battle of Verdun. He died in 1943, surviving long enough to experience the London Blitz in the early part of the Second World War, and writing the poem 'The Burning of the Leaves', which many think is his masterpiece: 'Nothing is certain, only the certain spring'.

Most people know the fourth stanza of 'For the Fallen', which forms an integral part of British Remembrance Sunday services and is also a central part of the Anzac Day services in Australia and New Zealand, and of the 11th November Remembrance Day services in Canada. It is a tribute to all those who give their lives in war, for whatever the country. The words of the poem echo the words of Adam in the Book of Genesis – 'Flesh of my flesh' becomes 'Flesh of her flesh', for England's dead children – and Shakespeare's 'Age shall not wither her' (referring to Cleopatra) becomes 'Age shall not weary them'.

A 1901 portrait of Binyon in pencil by William Strang is held at the National Portrait Gallery in London, and three of his poems – 'The Fourth of August', 'To Women' and 'For the Fallen' – were set by Sir Edward Elgar in his last major work for chorus and orchestra, *The Spirit of England*.

Address Between Pentire Head and The Rumps | Getting there Car park at Lead Mine, Polzeath, Wadebridge, PL27 6QY, from where it is a mile-long walk along dedicated footpaths | Hours Unrestricted | Tip The Rumps is the site of an Iron Age promontory fort with three ramparts built on a narrow strip of land and surrounded by the sea.

51 The Fishermen Statue

When the fish are gone, what are the Cornish boys to do?

Fishing has been a way of life for Cornish folk, probably since the first Stone Age people made their way from what is now the European continent and found a source of seafood in nearly every direction they could see! But supplying fish is now an important industry, with Newlyn a major fishing port.

Fishing is and always has been a hard life: towing the bottom trawl for three hours at a time, avoiding wrecks, in the rolling sea or the calm sea, at day over the grey waves and under the grey sky, on still nights with phosphorescence, hoping for a good catch. Gutting the fish as the boat steams to harbour; standing at the bow with the line ready to throw to the guy on the harbour wall as the boat comes to. This is a dangerous world, especially on a rolling boat, with the warps to the winch running across the aft deck to the gantry at the stern, and nets ready to catch your fingers. But many wouldn't have any other life.

This bronze statue by local sculptor Tom Leaper, was erected at Tolcarne in 2007 to honour these brave fishermen, especially those who lost their lives at sea. Called *Throw me a line*, this moving statue reminds the viewer of the peril of making a living on the sea. The fishing industry has always been full of superstition – women and the colour green used to be considered unlucky on the boats, but now women also take part in this different life, out on the sea, away from the sound of traffic and bustle in the towns, with the distant horizon for company.

Mining, the other major Cornish economy, didn't entirely pass by this corner of Cornwall; look eastwards along the shore line from the fishermen's statue on a spring low tide and you may see a small rocky outcrop covered in dense kelp seaweed some 240 yards from shore, all that remains of the unusual but briefly successful Wherry mine of the late 1700s, abandoned after storm damage in 1798.

Address 2 Lower Art Gallery Terrace, Newlyn, Penzance, TR18 5PP | **Getting there** Behind the Newlyn Art Gallery; limited parking at the end of Creeping Lane; also accessible on the South West Coast Path | **Hours** Unrestricted | **Tip** Newlyn Art Gallery (at New Road, Newlyn, TR18 5PZ) is just 76 yards inland from the statue, and has changing exhibitions of contemporary artwork, and a lovely café overlooking the sea.

52 Maen Cottage
Faraway Fancies

From his mid-terrace granite house in Elms Close Terrace just off Chywoone Hill, Harold Harvey could look over Newlyn and Penzance with a panoramic view to the sea. From his home, where he lived with his wife Gertrude (his former model and an accomplished artist herself), he could plan his paintings of Cornish fishermen, miners, farmers, housewives and places, such as *Faraway Fancies* (1921) a portrait of a young girl with a bright ribbon in her hair, in front of Newlyn Harbour, with the sea waves portrayed in green dashes.

Harvey was the best-known native-born Cornishman of the Newlyn School, made famous by artists such as Walter Langley and Stanhope Forbes. Artists were attracted by the everyday lives of the harbour, the boats, the fishermen and the fisher wives, as well as the light, made brighter by the reflections from the sea that surrounds the Cornish peninsula.

The Newlyn School was just getting established as Harvey, born in Penzance in 1874 and the son of a bank manager, was growing up; he trained at the Penzance School of Arts and later in Paris. He exhibited locally and at the Royal Academy, but like many Cornishmen preferred to stay in Cornwall – and who could blame him! There was so much to paint here: there are oil paintings of the local gentry, the tin miners of St Just, the Wheal Reeth tin mine at Breage, the china clay pit at Leswidden, even a lovely 1923 painting of the reeds at Marazion Marsh looking east towards the railway bridge high above the marsh, but most especially the lads and men in their boats, and the women in the their houses, and on the cliffs picking blackberries and apples.

Harvey died in Newlyn on 19 May, 1941 and is buried in the Roman Catholic section of St Clare Cemetery, Penzance; the slate inscription set in granite gives his full name: *Harold Charles Francis Harvey*.

Address Elms Close Terrace, Penzance, TR18 5AU | **Getting there** Going up Chywoone Hill in Newlyn, Elms Close is on your right | **Hours** Viewable from the outside only | **Tip** Westwards over the hill from Newlyn is 'Lamorna', famous in the early 19th century for the presence of Sir Alfred Munnings, Samuel John 'Lamorna' Birch, Dod Proctor and the Knights (Laura and Harold).

53 Ordnance Datum

Looking at an OS map? Think of Newlyn

Located on the end of the old pier in Newlyn Harbour is Newlyn Tidal Observatory, established in 1915 and one of the most important installations in the history of British mapping. It houses the marker against which the heights we see on land maps were originally measured. Mapping had shown only horizontal distances until the mid-1800s, when the measuring of heights began with the study of the shape of the earth. Reference levels were created at several sites but another survey showed that these varied, so the UK Ordnance Survey decided to create a single reference point. Newlyn pier was selected to record tidal level every 15 minutes, 24 hours a day, 365 days a year, continuing from 1915 to 1921. From this data, the mean level was marked with a brass bolt that remains to this day, and which became the benchmark for all land height readings in England and Wales, now known as Ordnance Datum Newlyn.

The observatory is now a Grade II-listed building. Inside there is a shaft, connected to the sea, in which the gauge equipment shows the level of the water as the tides rise and fall. The building withstood the violent storm of 1962 that devastated the harbour, the only day when no-one could reach it to take readings. In 1941 the gauge recorded the small tsunami that followed an earthquake west of Portugal. Sadly, the observatory is closed to the public, but it is hoped that funding will be secured for much-needed repairs.

GPS technology has now replaced the direct reference to Newlyn, but it's worth noting that when the Newlyn elevations were checked digitally they were found to be only a few centimetres out. And all that data hasn't been shelved – the measurements from the Newlyn Observatory have shown that the sea level rose, on average, 1.83 mm per year between 1915 and 2015, but at 3.8 mm per year between 1993 and 2014. ODN is still used for altitude measurements, such as Above Ordnance Datum (AOD).

Address 2 Strand, Newlyn, Penzance, TR18 5HW | Getting there Walk along the main harbour quay and the Observatory is on the end of the small quay opposite | Hours Currently closed awaiting repair work | Tip Newlyn still has a vibrant fishing industry – and a fish festival – but some of its older buildings have been converted to interesting other uses such as the Newlyn Filmhouse, a restaurant-cinema showing both big screen and local interest films.

54 The Huer's Hut
Heva, Heva now the catch is in, let the troyl begin

The main market for salted barrels of pilchard used to be Europe, particularly Italy, and there was good money to be made. In the good old days you'd get 3,000 fish in a barrel, plus the fish oil for lamps in houses and on streets. The huer was the lookout on the cliffs, living in the huer's hut from dawn to sunset, watching the sea for the ripple of shoals, or a darkening of the sea as the fish swarmed at the surface, or the frantic aggregations of diving sea birds. The shoals used to appear in huge numbers in late summer or early autumn as they followed the currents northwards. When a shoal was seen, the huer would wave gorse bushes and shout *Heva, Heva* across the town. He had to remain alert, keeping watch all day in season and on clear moonlit nights when the pilchards swam closer to the surface; you couldn't afford to miss a shoal. Once the shoal was spotted, the huer would direct the fishermen to where the shoal was moving. The boats would work together using seine nets deployed in a horseshoe shape like a wall around the shoal.

One hundred years ago the pilchards disappeared. Why did they die out? Was it over-fishing or changes to sea currents? They are back now, but only in small numbers. Renamed 'Cornish sardines', they are the same fish – small, tasty, and healthy, being high in omega 3 oils; other uses for pilchard oil have all but disappeared, and the Cornish sardine is now a sustainable industry.

The huer's hut is now redundant, but the Grade II-listed, 19th-century building on the headland at Newquay is a reminder of this unpredictable industry.

Nowadays, of course, fishermen have mobile phones and GPS, and the shoals are found using sonar. Small mesh ring nets are shot from small fishing boats out of Mevagissey and Newlyn, and the fish are packed in ice to keep them fresh. Look out for Cornish sardines in your local market.

Address King Edward Crescent, Newquay, TR7 1EN, www.what3words.com/ guidebook.dangerously.played | Getting there From the Atlantic Hotel the huer's hut is on the north (seaward) side by the road | Hours Accessible 24 hours | Tip Fistral Beach is generally acknowledged to be the home of British surfing, with a consistent high-quality surf and the Cribbar, where a huge wave (up to 40 feet) is created by an outcrop of rocks under the water, just to the west of the headland here.

55 Lappa Valley
Modern mining railway

The narrow gauge Lappa Valley Railway runs on one of the oldest railway track beds in Cornwall. The former East Wheal Rose branch line was first used on 26 February, 1849 as a horse-drawn tramway branching off from the Newquay to St Dennis line, designed and constructed by the same Joseph Treffry who was responsible for Treffry Viaduct. Now covering over 35 acres, trains travel on a 15-inch gauge line through a wooded valley to the old mining area, where you will find a boating lake, adventure golf course, play areas for children, a café and a separate miniature (7.25-inch gauge) railway. It is hard to believe that this area full of children playing was once the scene of a major mining disaster.

On 9 July, 1846 torrential rain fell during a tremendous thunderstorm, and torrents of water poured down the East Wheal Rose mine shafts; a gale of wind blew out the candles, leaving the miners in complete darkness. Amongst acts of heroism that day, Samuel Bastion lay across a manhole, diverting the flow of water and saving eighteen men. Thirty-nine others lost their lives; they are commemorated today by a plaque next to the Engine House of the still-flooded East Wheal Rose North Shaft, which is approximately 960 feet deep.

In 1874, the tramway was taken over by the Cornwall Minerals Railway, with steam locomotives replacing the horses. Twenty-two years later the Cornwall Minerals Railway was taken over by the Great Western Railway; the branch line was upgraded and became part of a new route from Chacewater to Newquay. But in the early 1960s Dr Beeching recommended the closure of this branch line as passenger numbers declined due to the increased popularity of the car, and the last standard gauge train puffed along the rails here on 4 February, 1963. In 1973, Lappa Valley bought the old railway line and developed it into the tourist site you can visit now.

Address St Newlyn East, Newquay, TR8 5LX, www.lappavalley.co.uk | Getting there Follow the signs from St Newlyn East | Hours Check the website for seasonal opening hours | Tip For railway lovers there is another privately owned heritage railway at Helston (www.helstonrailway.co.uk), a small volunteer-run project with about a mile of standard gauge track on which they run steam and diesel engines throughout the summer season.

56 Doom Bar
Not the beer – the real thing!

The mouth of the Camel estuary is beautiful and fascinating: visit on a sunny summer's day and it is a glorious spread of sandy beaches, coves and blue seas; visit on a stormy winter's day and you will see earth's natural forces at work in front of you.

The aptly named Doom Bar is definitely something to view from a distance. Lying at the mouth of the Camel estuary opposite Daymer Bay, it has always been the peril of the north coast for mariners. The surface of this bar of sand lies just below the water; if you look out to the estuary mouth you realise you are watching waves breaking where you wouldn't expect them. This is the trap for the unwary sailor heading for harbour; sailing vessels that round Stepper Point lose the wind in its shelter then drift helplessly onto the bar. Some survive, many don't, and in a stormy sea the waves breaking on the bar can be huge.

When you look further into the estuary you realise the Doom Bar isn't the only sand bar; this is a clue to the vast slow forces that govern our planet. Far from being static, these banks are on the move; the channel that ran alongside Hawker's Cove shifted to the east in the early 20th century so that the Doom Bar has moved from one side of the estuary to the other. Not only that, the banks of marine sands, made of billions of shell fragments, are moving very slowly further into the estuary (give or take the millions of tons that man has extracted for farming), working their way onto the bars, the beaches and the dunes.

Today the channel is dredged for safety but Doom Bar is still a treacherous place. Such is its importance it is also the stuff of legend. It is said that Doom Bar was inflicted on Padstow by a dying mermaid after she was shot by a local lad; the reasons given for his murderous act vary, but the mermaid's revenge has been all too effective – ships have been wrecked on Doom Bar for centuries.

Address The seaward end of the Camel Estuary | Getting there To get a good view of the estuary, climb to a highpoint on the southwest coast path near the sea on either side of the estuary | Hours View from a distance only – it is too dangerous to access | Tip This area of the coast has lots of geological interest, including the cliffs at Trebetherick that show sands compressed to rock, 'boulder beaches' and raised beaches.

57 Prideaux Place

Padstow's Elizabethan manor

If you've read any Rosamunde Pilcher or Winston Graham, or seen the TV series *Poldark*, you should visit this ancient country house near the Cornish coast. Captain Ross Poldark was seen galloping across the grass-covered north Cornish cliffs here and visiting the house itself. Winston Graham often stayed here; the manuscript of his final novel *Bella Poldark*, written here, was nearly lost in a serious house fire.

The house is most famously associated with Cornish-born author Rosamunde Pilcher; no fewer than 14 of her stories have been filmed here for German speaking countries, including *End of Summer (Das Ende eines Sommers), Winds Across the Sea (Winde über dem Meer)* and *The Woman on the Cliff (Die Frau auf der Klippe)*. The owner of the house appeared in some of these films, including as a chauffeur, gin taster and a coroner, rather as Alfred Hitchcock always appeared in his own films in small cameo roles.

Fancy living in the same house for 431 years? Fancy an estate with the same name as your family? Fancy having family links with William the Conqueror, King Edward I and Jane Austen? This house has been owned by 14 generations of the Prideaux-Brune family since its completion in 1592! They must like it. The 81-room house lies on the south bank of the Camel River and sits in an estate of over 3,460 acres. The house is a mix of different periods, and the great chamber above the hall has a fine-quality, circa-1600 plaster barrel vaulted ceiling, restored in the 1980s. The garden dates back at least to the 1730s and now has an 80-tree lime avenue, a remodelled Victorian formal garden, a hornbeam allée and woodland walks. There is also a large herd of fallow deer here, including the menil variety, probably one of the oldest park herds in the country The restoration of the garden has been carried out in association with the Lost Gardens of Heligan.

Address Prideaux Place, Padstow, PL28 8RP, https://prideauxplace.co.uk | Getting there The house is signposted from the A 389 in Padstow | Hours Café and gardens Mon – Fri 10.30am – 4.30pm; regular guided tours of the house Apr – early Oct Mon – Fri 11am – 3pm | Tip The National Lobster Hatchery, South Quay, Padstow, PL28 8BL, (www.nationallobsterhatchery.co.uk), is a marine conservation, research and education charity open to the public daily 10am – 4pm.

58 Dolly Pentreath

My ny vynnav kewsel Sowsnek

*Gwra perthi de taz ha de mam mal de dythiow bethenz hyr war an try neb an arleth de dew ryes dees** reads the memorial stone to Dolly Pentreath, a Cornish fishwife thought to be the last native Cornish language speaker. It is said that she refused to speak English and that she had only a few words of this foreign tongue; although it is not known how much Cornish she could actually speak, it was agreed that she could swear in Cornish!

Dolly died in 1777. Eighty-three years later this impressive memorial to her was set into the churchyard wall by Prince Louis Lucien Bonaparte (nephew of Napoleon), who spent a lot of time in England and studied dialects and languages. There is a plaque on the house in Brook Street, Mousehole, where Dolly lived, and a painting of her by John Opie in St Michael's Mount.

Today there is a great Cornish language revival, showing pride in Cornish history and identity. Cornish – or Kenewek – is taught in some schools and evening classes, and every year the Pennseythen Gernewek – Cornish Language Weekend – is held at different venues around Cornwall for everyone ranging from beginners to fluent Cornish speakers. For learners there are four exams – from First to Fourth Grade – run by the Cornish Language Board, and excellence at the language is one pathway to becoming a Bard of the Cornish Gorsedd (Gorsedh Kernow).

Ironically, the largest Cornish Festival in the world is probably in Australia, where Kernewek Lowender celebrates the presence there of the Cornish diaspora, the descendants of the Cornish miners who spread across the world. Most people know some Cornish words, even if they are only place names such as 'Carn Brea' – 'Rocky Hill' in English.

*Honour thy father and thy mother that thy days may be long upon the land which the Lord thy God giveth thee.

HERE LYETH INTERRED
DOROTHY PENTREATH
WHO DIED IN
1777,
SAID TO HAVE BEEN THE
LAST PERSON WHO CONVERSED
IN THE ANCIENT CORNISH
THE PECULIAR LANGUAGE OF
THIS COUNTY FROM THE
EARLIEST RECORDS
TILL IT EXPIRED IN THE
EIGHTEENTH CENTURY
IN THIS PARISH OF
SAINT PAUL

Address St Pol de Leon, Mousehole Lane, Paul, TR19 6TZ | Getting there The memorial stone is set in the church wall facing the road, opposite the King's Arms | Hours Unrestricted | Tip The church houses the memorial to the eight men of the Penlee Lifeboat who were tragically lost in 1981 trying to rescue the crew of the coaster Union Star on the coast off Mousehole.

59 Geevor Tin Mine

Put on your hard hat and down we go

Driving along the spectacular north coast road you may catch sight of a miner wielding his pick; he marks the entrance to Geevor where tin and copper were extracted. Laid out in front of the arriving visitor are the elements of mining as it was when this mine closed on 16 February, 1990. Geevor feels as if it is clinging on to the very edge of Cornwall. Steep rocky cliffs mark the seaward edge where the industrial landscape gives way to the romantic seascape, but even these cliffs show the mining legacy, with a bright slash of green-blue staining where the copper has oxidised in water from the mine.

Geevor is the site of Wheal Mexico, 'wheal' being the Cornish for mine or quarry. Wheal Mexico was dug and worked by mining men 200 years ago when their wives and daughters, the Bal Maidens, would have worked above ground breaking up the ore. It doesn't require too much imagination to feel as if you are back in the 1900s, when the mine was still working, and by the time you leave you may have walked through some of those underground tunnels with your hard hat on. Above ground the bare landscape speaks of the metals that lie locked into the soils and restrict the growth of plants.

One of the best pasties you will sample in Cornwall is the fine offering in the Count House Café here, not only for the quality of the pasty ('tis a proper job') but for its spectacular setting with a view straight onto the Atlantic – you can taste the salt in the air on a windy day. Despite the hardship that the loss of mining jobs brought to Pendeen, there was enough community foresight and drive to gather abandoned equipment, repair the buildings and develop the archaeology, geology and biodiversity of the site to add to the experience of the awe-inspiring industrial heritage. Geevor continues to be a community project with something for everyone.

Address Pendeen, Penzance, TR19 7EW, www.geevor.com | Getting there The entrance to Geevor mine is 0.3 miles west of the centre of Pendeen; buses 18, A17 and A3 (summer only) stop at the mine | Hours Mine Sun–Thu 10am–4pm (last entry 3pm); café Sun–Thu 9am–4pm; grounds accessible 24 hours | Tip Nearby is the Levant Mine, a National Trust property, the site of a terrible mining tragedy that adds a powerful thread to the dangers and hardship of a miner's life.

60 Enys Gardens
Oh, what a beautiful sight!

You hear this every spring as people walk beyond Enys House to where the native bluebell has produced a stunning field of azure blue. This is one of nature's glories, on warm afternoons filling the air with honey scent and the buzz of bees. Native bluebells are a dwindling treasure that is threatened by the invasion of the less elegant Spanish bluebell from misguided planting in gardens. Half of the world's population of native bluebell grow in the UK and to control their decline the native English bluebell, scientifically *Hyacinthoides non-scripta*, is protected by law. It is invasive in the garden but has an interesting past use – the sticky root sap was used to stiffen the muslin of Tudor collar ruffs and for fixing flight feathers to archers' arrows in the Middle Ages. Nowadays the sheer beauty of massed bluebells is quite enough to earn its place in our landscape (though badgers think them better used as bedding and food!).

The bluebell field, Parc Lye, is part of informal gardens begun in the early 19th century by Francis Enys, replacing Italianate gardens, the spirit of which remain. The gardens are believed to be the oldest in Cornwall, and include many fine tree specimens including the second largest maidenhair tree in the UK and introductions from Victorian expeditions. The small lake in the valley has a long history, including providing a reservoir of water to be pumped up to the house in case of fire. The orchard, started in 2012, echoes the Enys past as a treasury of Cornish apple varieties including the Cornish Aromatic.

Nowadays Enys is one of Cornwall's lesser-known private estates, but the Enys family has long been part of the history of Cornwall: Robert de Enys appears in records in 1272 and the estate and house have always been owned by the Enys family. The family name was even used by Winston Graham for the good Dr Dwight Enys in his *Poldark* novels.

Address Enys House, St Gluvias, Penryn, TR10 9LB, www.enysgardens.org.uk | Getting there By car, drive into Penryn on the B 3292, turn left at the bottom of the hill up Truro Hill, and Enys is about 1,750 yards on your right | Hours Gardens open Apr–Sep Sun & Mon 10am–5pm, with the bluebells in flower in May (check website for calendar); house viewable from outside only | Tip As historically important Cornish towns go, Penryn outstrips Falmouth. Its medieval remains include a wall and arch of Glasney College, founded in 1265, which was the religious centre of Cornwall until Henry VIII's dissolution of the monasteries.

61 Admiral Benbow
Yo ho ho, me hearties!

As character pubs go you would struggle to beat this one. This pub restaurant celebrates the history of the seafaring life – and not just pirates: from the beautifully carved front door to Lady Hamilton's Bar overlooking the harbour, there is much to spark your curiosity. It feels a little like a miniature theme park, but of course these objects – the canon and the rest – are real.

The present day pub is the creation of Roland (Roly) Morris, a keen diver and salvageman, who put together an amazing range of maritime artefacts from shipwrecks to decorate the interior, rein-venting it as a unique bar and restaurant. It is said that in the 1800s, when this pub was known as the Benbow, it was an illegal establish-ment frequented by smugglers and was the inspiration for Robert Louis Stevenson's Admiral Benbow. Even the roof is interesting – aside from the Cornish flag you can see, astride the roof top, a model of Octavius Lanyon, head of the Benbow Brandy Men, who smug-gled high-value goods to bring in some extra money in what were hard times.

This is not the only Admiral Benbow in the UK but it's proba-bly the one that comes nearest to the inn created by Robert Louis Stevenson in *Treasure Island*, where the hero Jim Hawkins grew up and where Billy Bones, the old sea dog, hid the secret to finding Treasure Island. The real Admiral Benbow was in fact a true hero, a multi-talented, ruthless fighting sailor who, in the late 1600s, took on the lawless privateers from France and the Barbary Corsairs who were capturing people for the North African slave trade. Piracy had become a very real problem for Mount's Bay, privateers swooping on Penzance and Newlyn, capturing and enslaving men, women and children for the Arab slave markets. Not something to celebrate, you would think, but that is where the inspiration for Gilbert and Sulli-van's operetta *The Pirates of Penzance* came from!

Address 46 Chapel Street, Penzance, TR18 4AF, www.thebenbow.com | Getting there Limited parking is available in Chapel Street; short- and long-stay parking on the harbour quay at TR18 2JX | Hours Tue–Sun noon–11pm; check website for food service hours | Tip Further along the coast at Falmouth is the National Maritime Museum Cornwall, a treasure trove of all things maritime Cornish, complete with piracy activities for kids, lectures, a library and a canteen with window seats overlooking Falmouth harbour!

62 Egyptian House
Walk like an Egyptian

Truly memorable shop fronts are few and far between, so that finding one where the original owner has gone to town is always a joy. You won't be expecting to find an impressive use of Egyptian symbology on a building in Cornwall but here we are in Penzance on a narrow street above the harbour. After the Napoleonic wars it was madly fashionable across Europe to replicate decorative elements of Egyptian architecture and it seems Cornwall was no exception. The Egyptian House in Penzance is a rare survivor of the style, the others from that era having been lost to urban modernisation.

What you see is in fact a façade placed over the frontage of two cottages in Chapel Street by then owner John Lavin in 1835. Even more than today the frontage would have been wildly unusual and exciting, and no doubt created to attract the attention of customers to the shop it decorated. Carrying the name Lavin's Museum, in the 1850s the shop sold rock and mineral specimens – Mr Lavin had ready access to a rich source of material from the miners of Cornwall, where the geology was (and still is) of special interest.

The frontage has changed very little since it was created, and just walking into the shops behind the façade has an exotic feel, although the merchandise may struggle to live up to the glorious entrance nowadays. The decorations are stylised but clearly show their Egyptian inspiration in the fine columns topped by capitals styled as lotus buds. Above the entrance you see a winged sun disc, a symbol for the sun god that is actually more Phoenician than Egyptian, the female heads suggesting the Egyptian goddess Hathor; at the top is the Royal Coat of Arms used by kings George III, George IV and William IV.

And to add to the fun you can actually stay in the building; the Landmark Trust has apartments available on each of the three floors above the shops.

Address Chapel Street, Penzance, TR18 4AW | Getting there The house is towards the top of Chapel Street, near the centre of Penzance | Hours Exterior accessible 24 hours | Tip Chapel Street sits in the oldest part of Penzance, and is laden with tier upon tier of history. Here you will find the Union Hotel, where the death of Nelson and his triumph at the Battle of Trafalgar were announced to England by a local fisherman.

63 The Gold Pillar Box
From gold medal to gold post

Easily missed on Quay Street, near the oldest part of Penzance harbour and in sight of the sea, is the post box painted gold to celebrate the Olympic medal won in 2012 by that great athlete, the rower Helen Glover MBE. A commemorative first-class stamp was also issued showing Helen and her rowing partner, Heather Stanner. Winner of two Olympic golds and three times a world champion, Helen has won many awards, but this has to be one of the most curious honours.

Born and raised in Cornwall, Helen was a natural athlete – and still is. She was born in Truro and grew up in Penzance and her great-grandfather started the famous Jelbert's ice-cream business in Newlyn where the recipe is a family secret (though it's no secret how delicious it is!).

There are in fact 110 gold pillar boxes in Britain and this one is not the only one Cornwall boasts. The sporting sons and daughters of Cornwall have the sea in their blood, and watersport is one of their strengths (though Rugby and Cornish Wrestling also feature highly) – maybe the modern manifestation of the pirate spirit! The letterbox in the wall of the Pandora Inn has been turned gold to celebrate the Olympic gold medal won by yachtsman Sir Ben Ainslie, who attended Truro School and, from a young age, learnt his sailing skills on Restronguet Creek in the Fal estuary. Ed Coode, born near Bodmin, went on to win gold in the 2004 Olympic coxless fours rowing team (but it seems there is no gold box for him).

The Royal Mail, which owns the boxes, intended to eventually return them to the standard pillar box red but the public voiced their outrage so we now keep our gold pillar boxes and the plaques that have been added to them. It is said that Helen Glover's gold box carries the distinction of having been the first one painted by the Royal Mail.

Address Quay Street, Penzance, TR18 4BD | **Getting there** By car, drive south along the quay by Penzance Harbour and just before you reach the South Pier, Quay Street is on your right | **Hours** Unrestricted | **Tip** Visit the Pandora Inn on the riverside at the mouth of Restronguet Creek; as well as the usual eating and drinking pastime you can take part in 'crabbing' on the edges of the pontoon – a favourite pastime for kids.

64___Hoxton Special
Laid back retro meets kite surfing

Seaside cafés are always great places, but the Hoxton Special is indeed special. Perched on the promenade above Marazion beach, here you can sit outside the charming tiny café (a former life-guard hut) and with your freshly made coffee or your Cornish cream tea (the tea comes in real china cups) take your ease. The wide sweep of Mount's Bay is laid out in front of you; the busy port of Penzance lies to your right, with Newlyn, Mousehole and the Carn-du headland beyond; and on your left is the ancient market town of Marazion, with Lizard headland in the distance. In front of you is a sandy beach and the imposing island of St Michael's Mount – tall and dark against the skyline. At high tide you can see the ferry taking people across to the island or at low tide watch a line of walkers stretched out along the paved causeway.

Now known as St Michael's Way, Hoxton Special sits on what is thought to be the route that pilgrims took from the north to the south coast of the county to reach St Michael's Mount, winding their way between the uplands of West Penwith and Godolphin Hill to avoid the treacherous seas off Land's End. Nowadays this part of the route is a busy multi-user track running alongside trains on the Great Western Main Line from Penzance to Paddington, just beyond the fence. Cyclists and walkers pick their way between each other on a surfaced track but everyone is generally friendly.

Hoxton Special is ideally placed for a stop off if you have walked or cycled from Penzance and, if you are feeling energetic, you can learn to kite surf, paddle a kayak or try the latest craze of stand-up paddle boarding. The calm sheltered waters of Mount's Bay are ideal for beginners, and the Hoxton Special staff provide expert tuition for all levels of expertise, followed by good food as a reward. The guys here have been voted one of the Top 10 Beach Bars and Cafés in Europe.

Address Beach Road, Marazion, TR17 0EW, www.thehoxtonspecial.com | Getting there
The nearest car park is at Marazion, TR17 0DA, just 164 yards away, but you can access
St Michael's Way from a range of places along the coast | Hours Thu–Mon 10am–4pm |
Tip The beautiful RSPB nature reserve of Marazion Marsh is just beyond the railway and
main road here; with binoculars you can see birds such as grey herons stalking amongst
the reeds, sea birds on the open water, and, in late autumn, flocks of starlings gathering
in huge numbers.

65 Humphry Davy Statue

'There's lots of things that I can do – I'm Humphry Davy'

Sir Humphry Davy's statue stands at the heart of Penzance looking eastwards, with a steady gaze; it is a tribute to an extraordinary Cornish scientist – at the forefront of chemistry in his lifetime – and his contribution to the progress of mankind. Born in Penzance in 1778, Humphry and his brother John looked to the exciting developments in science at the time for their careers, leaving behind country life. Davy described his rigid learning at the local grammar schools as 'a pain' whilst learning to investigate the natural world by himself. His career began whilst apprenticed to a local apothecary, he carried out experiments at home – much to the disgust of his family. By this time John had noted a 'genuine quality of genius' in his brother. On moving to Bristol in 1798 his career took off: on his way to receiving medals (one of which his wife threw into Mount's Bay), being knighted and becoming President of the Royal Institute in recognition of his achievements, he had found his purpose, revealing electrochemistry, and discovering chemical elements and anaesthetics, amongst other things.

Davy's travels to Europe brought international recognition and so well regarded was he that Napolean Bonaparte awarded him the Prix du Galvanisme while Britain was still at war with France. But he was also a poet, writer and artist, counting Samuel Taylor Coleridge amongst his friends and, with him, editing an edition of Wordsworth's *Lyrical Ballads*. In later years he famously invented a safety lamp for miners, many of whom had died when their naked flame lamps caused explosions. Look at the statue's right hand and you will see his lamp.

Today, the Davy Medal is awarded by the Royal Society for outstanding contributions in chemistry – awardees have also included Marie Curie. On the Saturday closest to his birthday, December 17th, the people of Penzance now celebrate their most famous son with a candlelit parade; there's even a song about him, he could do so many things.

Address The Market Building, Market Jew Street, Penzance, TR18 2TN | Getting there Easily found at the top of Market Jew Street | Hours Unrestricted | Tip Some of Davy's own paintings are in the Penlee Gallery.

66 The Jubilee Pool
Power to the people

This open air, natural seawater swimming pool is the largest in the UK and has just about everything you could wish for – regular refreshing from Mount's Bay, walls for shelter from brisk winds, open terraces for sunbathing, a good depth of water in the main pool, a children's pool, changing facilities and a decent café.

The pool is built on the Battery Rocks, a small rocky headland so named because a gun battery was installed there in 1740 to defend against French attack. The rocks were already a favoured bathing spot for tourists when the Jubilee Pool was built and remain a favourite spot for open water swimming – straight off the rocks into the water!

The main pool is not heated so you may think this is a bit close to wild swimming but there is a much warmer alternative – a smaller pool which is heated to about 30 degrees centigrade by the geothermal system bringing water from 450 yards (one and a half Eiffel towers!) below ground. You will need to book your hour slot to swim here, and the advice is to get out of the pool every 15 minutes to ensure you don't overheat! But even for non-swimmers Jubilee Pool is still worth a visit – it is a stunning art deco design, triangular in shape with clean uncluttered lines and gentle curves to its walls, and its views across the bay from the terrace are splendid. The pool is run as a social enterprise and there are also occasional events in the community space.

The Jubilee in question was King George V's Silver Jubilee in 1935 and the pool, much loved by local residents, has gone through a few crises in that time. But in recent years local energies have ensured its survival and restoration to its original glory and beyond, with the creation of the geothermal pool in 2020. A strong local community shareholding in the pool demonstrates the power of the community to influence local government and draw on grant support.

Address Jubilee Pool, Battery Road, Penzance, TR18 4FF, www.jubileepool.co.uk | Getting there On Battery Road just beyond Western Promenade Road; parking at St Anthony's long-stay car park across the road | Hours Check the website for details | Tip Cornwall boasts many other sea bathing pools on its coast, where the rocks have been adapted to create small tidal bathing pools, such as at Bude, Perranporth, Godrevy, Porthtowan, Looe (Millendreath), Mousehole and Kynance Cove.

67 Penlee Gallery
The rain it raineth every day

For a glimpse of how West Cornwall looked 100 years ago, you can visit Penlee Gallery to see paintings by members of the Newlyn School, the Lamorna Colony and other artists working in the area between 1880 and 1940. The Newlyn School artists usually worked directly from the subject, often in the open air (*en plein air*), using models from the fishing and farming communities.

Away from the mines, Cornwall was charmingly rural to the artists; the air was bright and soft and accommodation was cheap – those cheap days are long gone! What is still the same however is the weather. James Watt (of steam-engine fame) is quoted as saying 'When it rains in Cornwall it rains solid', and one of the highlights of the Gallery is the beautiful painting by Norman Garstin of the Penzance promenade in typical Cornish weather with sea spray, umbrellas, wet dogs and huddled children – *The rain it raineth every day*.

The Gallery displays paintings by other famous artists including Lamorna Birch, Elizabeth and Stanhope Forbes, Laura and Harold Knight, Harold Harvey, Dod and Ernest Proctor and Henry Scott Tuke, along with more modern art works and pieces of local historical interest.

There is still a thriving art scene in Cornwall and you may come across artists out in the country with their easels set up trying to catch the patterns and reflections of the sea. At the entrance to the Gallery is a sculpture by the contemporary artist Kurt Jackson of a Broccoli Juggler, representing the juggling act of Cornish farmers struggling to make a living.

The gallery building, Penlee House, is also home to the Penzance Natural History and Antiquarian Society collection, and as well as visiting the Gallery you can enjoy the adjacent Penlee Park with its sub-tropical plants, wooded areas and Memorial Garden, all in the heart of Penzance and open daily from 8am to dusk.

Address Penlee House, Morrab Road, Penzance, TR18 4HE, www. penleehouse.org.uk | Getting there There are several car parks in Penzance | Hours Mon–Sat 10am–5pm | Tip Morrab Gardens, with an entrance on lower Morrab Road, with its cast iron fountain, Victorian bandstand, Boer War Memorial statue, plentiful benches, subtropical plantings and elegant design is well worth a visit.

68   Penzance Swing Bridge
Mind the gap!

Walk along the harbour front in Penzance and you will come across a small bridge between the main harbour and a tiny inner harbour known as the Abbey Basin, and the entrance to the dry dock. This is an asymmetric swing bridge, created originally in 1881 using a redundant turntable from the nearby Penzance railyard. The bridge swings open sideways over a heavy metal table using a system of hydraulics to open the entrance to the inner harbour.

Wide enough at 44 feet to allow *Scillonia III* through, it's always an event when the bridge is being opened and, because this is quite a small structure, it is possible to stand and watch the whole operation from nearby. The Penwith local community radio station Coast FM (96.5 & 97.2FM in West Cornwall) provides notices of closures of the bridge, and the traffic that has ignored closure notices just has to wait! Interestingly the bridge opens from the western side because it closes onto a viaduct on the eastern side.

The bridge had a major overhaul in 1980 when it finally wasn't up to the increasing traffic load and the effects of the seawater. The local Visick's foundry undertook the work, and regular maintenance has been undertaken ever since. Known more formally as the Ross Bridge, it was named after Charles Campbell Ross, from Middlesex, of the nearby Morrab House, oft times Mayor of Penzance in the late 1800s and an MP.

The dry dock to which the swing bridge gives access is one of Europe's oldest, and one that has been used by Trinity House for refurbishment of the Trinity House Lightvessels, as well as maintenance for the Isles of Scilly Steamship Company ships. It's a lonely life for a Lightvessel; these are the unmanned warning vessels moored on hazardous areas for shipping. They carry fog horns and all the modern warning equipment. Currently, there is one moored on the Sevenstones reef to the west of Land's End.

Address Wharf Road, Penzance, TR18 4BW | Getting there Park in the main harbour car park, Penzance, TR18 2GB | Hours Accessible 24 hours; opens occasionally on demand when a ship needs to access the dry dock | Tip The Grade II-listed Abbey Warehouse at the side of the inner basin was built in the early 1800s. As a bonded warehouse it was used to store goods before the tax had been paid. A network of bricked-up smuggler tunnels was recently found under the Warehouse.

69 Submerged Forest
Trees under the sea

Anyone who has ventured into the wonderful tidal world between high and low water will know what wonders there are to be found there, but this is a quite different thing. Here you may find the stumps and roots of an ancient forest scattered amongst the rocks and rockpools.

This is a forest that in all likelihood spread across much of Mount's Bay, surrounding St Michael's Mount, called in Cornish 'Karrek Loos yn Koos' meaning 'grey rock in woodland'. The forest is 4,000 to 6,000 years old. Mount's Bay is one of the best places to see it as the lowest tides retreat (another is on the beach at Bude). The sand shifts with every tide though, so there are times when nothing is uncovered but others – especially after a storm – when there is much more.

Acquaint yourself with the tidal charts for Cornwall so you can time your visit for the lowest of the spring tides – say 1.3 feet ACD – which will be towards noon, and try for a day when the barometer shows rising pressure. Best equip yourself with wellies and then head out across the shore sand flats on the Penzance end of Marazion beach to the low dark rocks at the very edge of the retreating tide, to see if the sea gods are with you. Look for low dark mounds where there is little or no seaweed growth amongst the sand and rocks, then gently press a finger onto the wet surface. A spongy feel will tell you that this is indeed the ancient seawater-soaked remains of a tree and that you are standing where a forest once grew. Once you get your eye in you may find many more stumps and roots.

You won't be able to resist doing some rock pooling amongst the rocks and tree stumps. Here you may find a shanny, a shore crab or a pipe fish amongst the beadlet anemones hiding under the tough brown wrack seaweeds.

Address Penzance | Getting there Park at Long Rock car park and head west south west to the edge of the sea | Hours Accessible at extreme low tides only | Tip On a sunny summer's day, on a very low tide, it's great to wade out to the rocky outcrops of Longrock reef (or maybe get your snorkel out). In the water around the rocks you can see small fish and cuttle-fish, but wear beach shoes to protect your feet from stones and weever fish.

70__ The Turks Head
Pirates and smugglers

It has to be one of the most historic pubs in Cornwall. Built in the 1200s, at the time of the crusades, it even retains some original features. Turks Head pubs in England supposedly get their name from a link to the crusades but it seems just as likely that this pub's name has a link to the infamous Barbary Corsairs, the pirates who raided Penzance, Mousehole and Marazion, amongst many other coastal villages, in the 1600s. They were mostly North African and their bounty was men, women and children to be sold into the Arab slave trade.

But this small pub probably has more of a smuggling heritage, and the traditional interior is heavy with atmosphere, almost certainly because of the history in its walls, which will have overheard many a smuggling conspiracy in their time. Times were hard and though some smugglers probably went off to Bristol to join the notorious pirates sailing the high seas, smuggling was a way of life all round the Cornish coast till the 19th century. It was a desperate, often ruthless, and well-organised business; smuggling stories abound, the more noble of which were about ordinary folk trying to survive under heavy taxation and disappearing fish stocks. One such was 'Doga' Pentreath of Mousehole who was described by a local customs officer as 'an honest man in all his dealings though a notorious smuggler'.

Nowadays the pub prides itself on the local craft beers it offers, along with a selection of rums, and a good menu in the restaurant. You can sit inside to soak up the atmosphere or retreat to the little courtyard at the back, which has a secret: there was reputed to be a tunnel from the courtyard down to the old harbour (only a stone's throw away down the Abbey slipway); it would almost certainly have been used by smugglers to bring contraband gin, tobacco and brandy ashore in the days of the Excise men – a very different occupation to piracy.

Address 49 Chapel Street, Penzance, TR18 4AF, www.theturkshead.pub | Getting there Parking on Chapel Street, and on the harbour quay, TR18 2JX | Hours Daily noon till late | Tip Look around historic Chapel Street. The brick house with white pillars was the home of Maria Branwell, the mother of Emily, Charlotte and Anne Brontë. The Penzance Arts Club – well worth a visit – is housed in the former Portuguese Embassy.

71 Warrens Pasties
Oggy oggy oggy!

You can't visit Cornwall without tasting a Cornish pasty – the first ever convenience food, now with Protected Geographical Indication (PGI) status in Europe: if it's not made in Cornwall, it's not a Cornish pasty!

The traditional Cornish pasty is a mix of beef (traditionally skirt), potato, onion and turnip (the yellow kind, known elsewhere as 'swede'). Some of the best pasties are filled with steak. The ingredients are uncooked then covered with pastry, which is crimped along the edge. You can glaze the pastry with milk then into the oven it goes. The crimp serves as a handle so you can eat it with dirty hands: in the old days, tin miners' hands might have been covered with poisonous arsenic, so they would throw away the contaminated crimp and eat the rest. The pastry envelope needs to be soft enough to eat but strong enough so it can be carried around – in the old days down the mines, nowadays when you are out working or on holiday jaunts.

It is said that wives and sweethearts would shout down the mines *Oggy, oggy, oggy* to say that the pasties were ready, and the miners would shout back *Oi, oi, oi*; so at any Cornish gathering – in folk clubs, at Cornish dancing, at the choirs singing, at the rugby – when you hear the cry *Oggy, oggy, oggy* you know to yell back *Oi, oi, oi.*

Warrens claims to be the oldest Cornish pasty producer in the world, starting in 1860 in St Just with their own recipes when Miss Harvey, daughter of the St Just baker, met Master Warren, a local farmer's son. One family provided the pastry and baked the pasties, while the other family provided the filling. These recipes have been passed down the years and are still in use today. You can have the pasties in medium or large, traditional or a range of new-fangled versions – how about cheese and onion, chicken, or even vegetarian, vegan or gluten-free pasties? It all depends on your taste.

THE
OLDEST
CORNISH
PASTY MAKER
IN THE
WORLD

Address There are 18 Warrens bakeries in Cornwall; the photo was taken at Warrens Bakery, 85A Market Jew Street, Penzance, TR18 2LG, www.warrensbakery.co.uk | **Getting there** Park in the harbour car park, TR18 2GB, and take the elevator in the Wharfside Building | **Hours** Mon–Sat 9am–4pm, Sun 10am–4pm | **Tip** Try other Cornish specialities – saffron buns and saffron cake, Cornish splits, Cornish fairings and Cornish hevva cake.

72 St Piran

Black, white and gold on the golden dunes

On the Sunday nearest the national day of Cornwall, St Piran's Day, the 5th of March, a huge procession takes place across Penhale Dunes, come rain or shine, to celebrate Cornwall's patron saint, who sailed across the sea from Ireland in the 5th century. Legend has it that this Christian missionary was thrown over a cliff tied to a millstone, but did not drown; instead he floated over to Cornwall on a calm sea and landed at Perranporth.

Here he built his oratory, one of the oldest churches in Britain, the remains of which you can still see here, lying low in a dune hollow and often flooded with water. The procession stops in several places en route from the nearby holiday complex to watch little playlets that tell the story of St Piran. Everyone then climbs up to St Piran's Cross, eight feet high, with its three-holed wheelhead carved from a single piece of granite – perhaps the oldest Celtic stone cross in Cornwall.

St Piran is also the patron saint of tin miners, and is said to have re-discovered the art of tin smelting (although tin mining pre-dated his arrival here). The national flag of Cornwall, white on black, is said to represent white tin flowing from the black rock, or, for some, good overcoming evil.

Cornwall has its own Celtic language and had its border with Devon along the river Tamar fixed in 936, over 1,000 years ago. The St Piran's Day march across the dunes is a celebration of Cornwall's national identity, with flags flying, Cornish spoken and sung, Cornish bagpipes playing and Cornish tartan worn. Anyone can join, of any age; all are welcome, including the English and other foreigners. Wear white or black and gold and carry daffodils. As you walk, watch out for the national bird of Cornwall, the black chough, recently returned to Penhale Dunes, and easily distinguished by its red legs and beak.

Address Perranporth, TR4 9PN | Getting there Access by a footpath across Penhale Sands; the march leaves from the holiday camp | Hours Unrestricted | Tip St Piran's Old Church, a replacement building for the Oratory, has been excavated and can be seen near St Piran's cross, high on the dunes.

73 St Enodoc Church
Blesséd be St Enodoc

It is said that this church was buried in sand for over 200 years, and the vicar and congregation had to descend through a hole in the roof to hold services and keep the tithe payments coming in. But now you can walk here through the golf course in 10 minutes (look out for golf balls!). A hermit called St Enodoc was said to have lived here and the church, sited on the spot where he lived, dates back to the 12th century. Grade I-listed, the architecture is Early English with rubble walls, a slate roof and a Celtic cross in the porch. The crooked tower dates from the 13th century and houses a bell salvaged from the wreck of the Italian two-masted sailing ship the *Immacolata*; on 26 September, 1875, on a voyage from Corfu to Falmouth, she ran aground on Doom Bar and sank, though her eight crew survived.

The church, unearthed and renovated in 1864, stands solitary amongst the dunes, a place of quiet, protected from the Atlantic gales by the 200-foot-high Brea Hill. On stormy days the sand builds up against the walls, threatening to bury the church once again.

This site is perhaps best known as the burial place of John Betjeman, who held the honorary position of Poet Laureate from 1972 until his death in 1984. He spent his childhood at nearby Trebetherick (his father is also buried here) and bought a home overlooking the 12th hole of the golf course. He has always been connected to Cornwall and was the author of *Betjeman's Cornwall*. As an architectural conservationist, he fought to protect our town landscapes, including Walsingham Place in Truro, from the vandalism of 1960's town planners, and he campaigned successfully to save the magnificent St Pancras Station from destruction; there is a statue to him there. Amongst his poems – always easy to read and understand – is 'Sunday Afternoon Service in St. Enodoc Church, Cornwall': walk across the golf course, ignoring the golf but 'bound for God', past 'Red Admirals basking with their wings apart'.

Address Trebetherick, Wadebridge, PL27 6SA | **Getting there** Park in the Daymer Bay car park, PL27 6SA, and follow the signs to St Enodoc Church; access on foot only | **Hours** Daily 7.30am–dusk | **Tip** Rocky Valley (Tintagel, PL34 0BQ) has two labyrinths or mazes carved into the rock face behind a derelict 18th-century mill on the eastern banks of a small stream, in a lovely deep valley – are they Bronze Age, Celtic or 18th century?

74 South Crofty

When the tin is gone, what are the Cornish boys to do?

Tin mining is at the heart of Cornwall's history – along with fishing, mining runs deep in Cornish veins. This was shown by the huge public interest in South Crofty mine in 1994 when South Crofty plc was in financial trouble and hundreds of local people bought shares; the seal on the certificate was made from tin produced at the mine. It is likely that everyone knew the company would fail but this was an emotional not a financial transaction for the Cornish people.

The prosperity of the mine went up and down according to the price of tin, and the company changed hands many times over the years. The land was more valuable for development, and in the early years of the present century an attempt was made by developers and politicians to close the mine and develop the land for housing, leisure and business. Huge numbers of local people protested at this disregard for Cornish history and the attempt to turn this part of Cornwall into a characterless suburban wasteland, despite its location within the World Heritage Site of the Cornwall Mining Landscape. You used to be able to tour the Tuckingmill decline and come to the surface in a lift.

Mining has been carried out at South Crofty since 1592, working the Great Flat Lode, a mineral-bearing body of rock under the southern granite slopes of Carn Brea, over two miles long and lying at an angle of about 30 degrees in contrast to many lodes which lie at a deeper angle. You can still buy jewellery made from South Crofty tin – cufflinks, pendants, earrings, bracelets and rings. Current owners Cornish Metals, who have an Underground Permission valid until 2071, are investigating new rich tin lodes and the possibility of extracting lithium from brine as part of its water-pumping work. After all the ups and downs of recent years, South Crofty is still here, and hopefully the mine Head Gear will still be towering over Pool for many years to come.

Address South Crofty Mine, Dudnance Lane, Pool, Redruth, TR15 3QT | Getting there
Visible from the Tuckingmill Junction | Hours Viewable from the road 24 hours; no access
to the site | Tip Cornwall Underground Adventures run underground mining tours in
west Cornwall, from simple tours to advanced adventures for the brave, with abseiling,
exploration and caving ladders! Not for the claustrophobic.

75 Doyden Castle
Where Mrs Tishell proposed to Doc Martin

This lovely tiny Gothic castle sits high on the exposed sea cliffs of Doyden Point above Port Quin on the north coast of Cornwall. It was built in the 1830s by the wealthy Samuel Symons. Built of dressed granite with mullioned windows and a battlemented parapet, strong enough to withstand the Cornish gales, the house was sited here not for its beautiful views but because its isolation meant that no-one could tell what Symons was doing there.

Symons' parties went on for days; gambling and drinking on the top two floors, with his wine cellars in the basement. His guests came by horse or carriage along the narrow track from the road down to Port Quin. This tiny hamlet was for a time deserted after a great storm, when many men died whilst fishing and their families abandoned the village, leaving it a ghostly, lonely place.

Nowadays Doyden Castle is best known for its appearance on television. In the early BBC version of *Poldark* in 1975 it was used as the home of Dr Enys, but it now holds a special place in the ITV series *Doc Martin*, filmed in Port Isaac just 1.9 miles away, under the name of 'Portwenn'. The grumpy Doctor Ellingham has had a baby with his new wife Louisa, the village headmistress, but Sally Tishell, the village pharmacist, has a crush on the Doctor – so it is not a good move to ask her to mind their baby. She has self-prescribed some drugs which heighten her desire, and she rushes off with the baby to Doyden Castle, where she waits for the doctor. He has to talk the poor deluded woman down by pretending he loves her and is finally able to take his baby from her arms. The local policeman is dissuaded from arresting her, and she is led off, quiet and defeated, to get some badly needed help.

You can now rent the castle from the National Trust, but you'll have to join the queue – it is one of the most popular National Trust places to rent.

Address Port Quin, Port Isaac, PL29 3SU | Getting there Park in the small car park at 2 Fish Cellars, Port Quin, Port Isaac, PL29 3SU | Hours Viewable from the outside only | Tip The majority of the ITV *Doc Martin* production was filmed in the 14th-century fishing village of Port Isaac; here you can see Doc Martin's quaint Fern Cottage, but you can't go inside.

76 Guy Gibson

One of the most splendid of all our fighting men

These are Churchill's words. This is the man who carried out 172 flight operations in the Second World War, won the Victoria Cross (the highest award for bravery) and led the Dambusters on their famous raid with the bouncing bomb. Designed by Barnes Wallis to bounce on the surface of the water, the bombs destroyed the dams at the Mohne and Eder reservoirs on the night of 16–17 May, 1943. The planes flew dangerously low so that the bombs could be dropped from a height of just 59 feet at over 230 miles per hour, spinning backwards as they hurled across the water and down the dams to explode at their base.

It appears that little thought had been given to civilian casualties. The floods as the dams broke drowned up to 1,400 people in torrents of water up to 39 feet high – the event is called the *Mohnekatastrophe* in Germany. Fifty-three airmen were also killed. The third target dam, Sorpe, was undamaged and continued to supply water for the Ruhr, the industrial heartland of Germany.

Guy Gibson went to primary school in Penzance; his portrait hung in West Cornwall School for Girls, long since closed. After a brief spell in India his mother took him away from his father and home to Porthleven, her birthplace. She was an alcoholic, at one time sentenced to prison for driving offences, and died of burns when her clothes caught in an electric fire when she was drunk on Christmas Eve 1939; Gibson was just 21.

It is perhaps not surprising that he was unpopular with his fellow pilots, a lonely and bossy man who loved his black labrador and expected all men to be as brave as him. His plane crashed and lit up in flames at Steenbergen in the Netherlands in 1944. There is a bronze plaque to him on the Bickford Smith Institute in Porthleven, a street named after him (Gibson Way) and a memorial cenotaph in Porthleven Cemetery.

DEDICATED TO THE MEMORY OF
W/Cdr GUY GIBSON
V.C. D.S.O. D.F.C. R.A.F
617 SQDN. THE DAMBUSTERS
ON THE 45TH ANNIVERSARY
OF HIS DEATH.
TUESDAY 19TH SEPTEMBER 1989

Address Porthleven Cemetery, Helston, TR13 9LJ | Getting there The cemetery is in the centre of Porthleven; Gibson Way is the first turning on the right as you arrive from Helston on the B 3304; the Bickford Smith Institute is the most prominent building in Porthleven with its 69-foot-high clock tower | Hours Accessible 24 hours | Tip Near the Old Lifeboat House, look out for sculptor Holly Bendall's life-size bronze sculpture of a man and a gull – *Waiting For Fish* – known locally as 'Dave and Bird'.

77 — Loe Bar

On one side lay the Ocean, and on one, Lay a great water…

It was here, almost certainly, that Alfred, Lord Tennyson walked across the shingle in 1848 and gained the inspiration to write *The Passing of Arthur*, in which he describes how Sir Bedivere, the solitary surviving attendant on King Arthur, throws the sword Excalibur into the lake. He tells how Sir Bedivere carries Arthur, wounded in his last battle, across the dewy pebbles between the lake and the sea. Arthur instructs him twice to throw the sword into the lake, but each time he hides it. On the third instruction he throws the sword and a mystic arm catches it by the hilt to draw it under the water; then a boat glides across the pool to carry Arthur to the Vale of Avalon.

The Bar's idyllic appearance on a sunny afternoon is deceptive; for all its beauty it has a dramatic and tragic history. If you visit you must be aware that it can be a dangerous place when the waves are high. The beach shelves steeply, shifting endlessly with a powerful and deadly backwash as the waves swell and retreat. People have drowned here, despite the signs – no swimming!

There have also been shipwrecks. On the walk down you pass a monument to HMS *Anson*, deliberately run aground after its anchoring cables broke in a storm; over 120 people were lost. On stormy nights, local people used to say 'the Bar is calling', the sound of drowned men calling out their names against the sea. In 1912, the 3,641-ton Italian *Tripolitania* was deliberately beached there in 100mph winds by running at full speed towards the Bar; all but one of her 28 crew were saved.

Despite all this, it is a magical place, with silvery sea holly everywhere and Loe Pool – the largest freshwater lake in Cornwall – a calm backdrop. The site was left to the National Trust on condition that it be kept 'a place of quiet beauty for people to enjoy without distraction'.

Address Chyvarloe, Helston, TR12 7PY, www.what3words.com/fabric.planting.unpainted | Getting there Park in the small car park just beyond Chyvarloe Farm and walk 875 yards down the track towards the sea | Hours Unrestricted | Tip One of the cannons from HMS *Anson* stands outside Helston Museum.

78 Porthleven Erratic – the Giant's Stone

Nice gneiss!

Long ago, it seems, the forces of nature decided to leave a stony curiosity on the Porthleven beach. Or maybe it was one of our Cornish Giants fooling around after a night out?

Lying incongruously on the flat rocky reef in this lovely cove just round the corner from the village is a huge rosy-orange boulder that has tested the imagination of geologists and storytellers alike. Technically for the geologist the boulder is a type of rock known as garnetiferous gneiss which forms when granite, which originated as molten magma deep within the earth, has been put under huge pressure several miles below the surface of the earth. Plenty of granites around in Cornwall, you say, but this boulder would have been born many, many miles away from Cornwall and the geologists seem certain it wasn't born anywhere in the UK.

So how did it arrive on this coast? The geologists believe that it was dropped here from floating ice in the period known as the Pleistocene when there were repeated 'Ice Ages' – although geologists don't agree about whether Cornwall was covered in ice in the last Ice Age. A geologist would call this out-of-place boulder an 'erratic' but it is known locally as the Giant's Stone or Moonstone. At an estimated 5 tons, it would have been a mighty giant that threw this boulder around, but even then – where did he get it from? Bad storms like the one in 1989 when waves crashed over Porthleven haven't shifted the stone. Did a tsunami sweep it in?

The stone is uncovered at low tide and sits on the very lowest level of the rocky reef, so keep an eye on the incoming tide if you walk out to inspect it at close quarters. Look very closely at the rock surface and you may be able to see the tiny flecks of garnet – a semi-precious stone formed by chemical changes due to the pressure on the granite.

Address Porthleven, TR13 9LA | Getting there Walk uphill from the Ship Inn, turn left onto Ocean View and follow the coastal footpath for about 437 yards; the erratic is down below you in the next cove | Hours Accessible at low water on spring tides | Tip If you look behind the boulder to the cliffs known as Pargodonnel Rocks you can see the rust-coloured remains of a beach that existed many millions of years ago, the beach sands cemented by iron and squashed between rocks contorted during geological history.

79 Lady Bassett's Baths
Hidden baths, surf and caves

It's not the wildest that Cornwall has to offer, but Portreath Beach is a great place; it's full of delights from the beach cafés and their pasties to pools carved into the rock, and the Atlantic Ocean's crashing waves.

There's an extensive beach in front of parking and a promenade. You can surf, swim, explore rock pools, or just sit on a bench and watch the summer lifeguards patrol the beach, and the surf lifesaving club training on the beach. A small stream runs across the beach to the sea; it's always a magnet for kids to build sandy dams. Or explore the rocks. The Mermaid's Pool is easy to find at low tide; cut into rock at the harbour wall, it is large enough to swim in.

More difficult to find at the other end of the beach are six small hand-cut baths cut into the steep cliffs. The highest one is near the small cave, another is in the seaward entrance to the cave. At least one should be usable at all tides.

A tiny mermaid might fit into any of these, but in fact they were built in the 1780s for Susannah, Lady Basset of Tehidy Park. Some were private; if you could climb the rocks, you could sit in these pools, take a salt water cure or just splash about in the water. The beach is next to Portreath Harbour, where a small fishing fleet brings in catches during good weather. Large waves barrel along the harbour wall, past the 'Monkey House', where lanterns were used to guide boats in, but the battering sea has made the wall dangerous.

After a day on the beach you can sit outside the licensed Atlantic Café with your food and drinks to watch the sunset over the sea. In winter the beach is wilder; seas move the beach on every tide, sometimes high, sometimes low. Look out for the fulmars returning to bag their nest sites for next spring, flying in stiff-winged from the sea to perch on the high cliffs at the back of the beach. A few hundred yards away is Gull Rock, crowded with seabirds.

Address Portreath Beach, TR16 4PH, www.what3words.com/spoken.dislikes.shipyards | Getting there Portreath is easy to find on the north Cornish coast | Hours The highest pool is accessible at all times, the lowest at very low tide | Tip Tehidy Country Park is the largest area of woodland in west Cornwall, with free car parks, woodland trails, a lake and a café. The north cliff car park is 1.5 miles west on the B 3301 between Porteath and Hayle.

80_Macsalvors

One stop shop for almost everything

Do you want to buy a deep-water diving bell (complete with dials and gauges) or a navigation light in its housing? How about a 12-cylinder 550 kilowatt-generating set or a jumbo crane? You're too late for the 12-tonne anchor from the aircraft carrier *Ark Royal* or the one from the Royal Yacht *Britannia* (sorry, they've been sold) and you're not allowed to buy the Royal Navy Mark 8 torpedo (wouldn't that be fun to play with!). Maybe you want to hire out one of their distinctive mobile truck-mounted orange cranes, which can regularly be seen trundling slowly up the steep A 30 hills; their largest one has a jib length of 300 feet.

Or maybe you need rubber matting? Or orange high viz clothing for work or to make you visible as you cycle along the narrow Cornish lanes at night. Or how about a garden spade, a piece of heavy chain for your boat, a few stainless steel screws, a desk for your office or even a genuine oak barrel direct from a whisky distillery (Scotch of course, as the 'Mac' in Macsalvors refers to the two Scotsmen who set up the business in 1957 as 'salvors', buying and selling Ministry of Defence surplus, dismantling and demolition work)?

The business dates back many years. In 1947, the Queen Elizabeth Class Warship HMS *Warspite* sank off Prussia Cove in Cornwall. The ship was refloated and beached along the coast at St Michael's Mount. This was the real start of the business. Then the Macs started their plant hire business in 1962 and have worked on several famous projects over the years, including the Earth Satellite Station at Goonhilly and the world-famous Eden Project.

Wherever you live in the world they can supply you (they have even sold Cornish shovels to Australia) but the best bet is to wander around the premises yourself and see what you want. You may even spot that thing you don't know the name of but you know you'll need one day!

Address Wilson Way, Illogan Highway, Redruth, TR15 3RS, www.macsalvors.com |
Getting there By car, leaving the A 30 at Tuckingmill, drive up the hill to the traffic light,
turn left past MacDonalds, and Macsalvors is on your right after about 0.6 miles | Hours
Mon – Sat 8am – 5.30pm, Sun 10am – 4pm | Tip Heartlands (Dudnance Lane, Pool,
TR15 3QY), just 0.3 miles away, is a 19-acre Cornish Mining World Heritage Site, a free,
family-friendly visitor attraction with a mining museum and exhibition, diaspora gardens
and an adventure playscape for kids.

81__Wellie Dogs
Woof woof!

Redruth celebrates its important mining heritage with cheerful street sculptures. In Tatty Square, the small town square on the steep hill of Redruth's main street, you come across this 'installation', which brings a smile to many a face. Although the small people who gleefully clamber over it won't be aware of its origin, it may well be one of the artist David Kemp's best-known local pieces. He works from his home near St Just on the West Penwith Peninsula but has produced iconic pieces in many of the post industrial areas of Britain including Old King Coal on an old railway path in County Durham.

David's USP is recycling 'stuff' for his work – it's amazing the inspiration he has found in ordinary objects, as well as redundant machinery – but the boots of the Hounds were no ordinary boots. He created these entertaining figures in bronze at the request of the local councils, basing them on the originals he had first produced from the discarded industrial boots of the working miners of Geevor Tin Mine after the mine closed, ending thousands of years of tin mining in Cornwall. Each Hound used seven boots. Officially known as the 'Tinners Hounds' they were installed in the heart of Redruth in 2006 as a tribute to Cornish miners.

Many Cornish miners left their native land to find work elsewhere in the world when Cornwall's mining economy collapsed, and so it is with the relatives of the Tinners Hounds; they have found homes in the Kelvingrove Art Gallery and Museum, and the Glasgow Museums Resource Centre.

Further up Fore Street you will see a rather different reminder of the town's mining history – the remarkable sculpted figure of a Cornish miner holding the pick tool and an ingot of tin, wearing the felt helmet with its candle and looking out to the future across the Redruth and Camborne Mining District.

Address 82 Fore Street, Redruth, TR15 2BL | Getting there From Fore Steet, turn right down the hill and you will see the sculptures just above the cinema | Hours Unrestricted | Tip Murdoch House at 7 Cross Street, Redruth, TR15 2BU, was the house of William Murdoch, one of the many famous Cornish inventors; amongst other things, this was the first building in the world to be lit by gas lighting.

82 The Ferryman Statue

Ferry across the Tamar

Saltash, the 'Gateway to Cornwall', may not be the most glamorous corner of Cornwall but it is rich in history, the first of the ports to establish on the Tamar estuaries, pre-dating Plymouth. The Saltash ferry, using oars and ropes, has crossed the Tamar since the Norman Conquest. In 1270, the feudal Baron Roger de Valletort sold the ferry rights to the Earl of Cornwall, earning the Earl £6 a year in rent. Without this ferry you had to travel up to Gunnislake to cross the Tamar. On the Devon side the ground needed to land the ferry was deemed the 'Cornish Patch', part of Cornwall until 1896 when it was officially transferred to Devon.

Stand on the Green on a sunny day and the river looks peaceful, but the current is strong: in 1733, the ferry capsized and sank, with the loss of 20 lives. In the 1830s, a chain ferry was introduced, making the crossing safer. After 1859, you could look up at the new Royal Albert railway bridge, designed by Isambard Kingdom Brunel; his statue stands on the nearby Green, looking over to Devon. The completion of the new suspension bridge closed the ferry on 23 October, 1961, with the loss to Saltash of the ferry revenue. Note that you only pay a toll when travelling out of Cornwall – returning is free!

Under the bridge is *The Saltash Ferryman*, a sculpture created by John Forster to honour the ferry and the ferrymen, with brass panels illustrating the ferry story over the centuries – all human life is here. Near Brunel's statue, you see the seated, life-sized figure of Ann Glanville. She was a tough woman, ferrying folk and goods about the river and racing pilot gigs with her all-woman crew, often beating the men's teams including the 10 best in France. Curiously a button in the middle of her chest states 'press her brooch to hear her story'. Today the Cornish tradition of gig racing is strongly upheld in Saltash and, what's more, they have an 'England and back' race!

Address Old Ferry Road, Saltash, PL12 4EH | Getting there By car, take North Road down the hill towards the river Tamar and park on the road by the small green; the Ferryman Statue, and the statues of Isambard Kingdom Brunel and Ann Glanville, are beneath the railway bridge | Hours Accessible 24 hours | Tip The Saltash Museum and Local History Centre at 17 Lower Fore Street is open year round and has a small permanent display about the history of Saltash, as well as temporary displays in summer.

83 Seaton Beach

Where the river Seaton meets the sea

Seaton Beach is where the river Seaton ('Seythyn' is Cornish, meaning 'little arrow river'), runs under the coast road and winds to the sea across the beach of grey sands eroded from the adjacent rocks. This is Cornwall's Seaton, not the upstart Devon version; it's a small village nestling at the sea end of a narrow, wooded valley. Storm waves occasionally reshape the beach and river bed, and sea defences have been put in place to protect the road and village.

In summer, children and dogs paddle in the shallow river, gulls cry overhead and families wait patiently for barbecues to heat up by the sea wall. Sometimes there is a café open at the beach top where you can shelter inside on stormy days and watch the waves crash onto the empty beach or take your drink out to a bench in the sunshine. At the end of the day you can stand at the tip of the sand bar, with the open sea on one side and the rushing river on the other to watch the sun set behind the looming dark of Looe Island, a Cornwall Wildlife Trust nature reserve.

Seaton is a great place to set off for a wildlife walk. In spring, the steep slatey cliffs to the west are brightened by the white and pink flowers of sea campion and sea thrift; along the coastal footpath to Looe in April you may spot the bright orange and black of a pearl-bordered fritillary butterfly as it dances over the cliff flowers, or in July, the marbled white butterflies flitting along the pathways, adjacent woods and fields. If you go early enough in the day you may be lucky enough to spot an adder basking quietly in the morning sunshine.

Just as appealing is the Seaton Valley Countryside Park that lies just across the road. From here you can escape the crowds and walk through oak woodland along nature trails by the river Seaton as far as Hessenford, looking for otter tracks in muddy places by the river, or exercising on the outdoor gym.

Address Seaton Beach, Looe Hill, Seaton, PL11 3JQ | Getting there Park at the entrance of the Country Park | Hours Accessible at all times | Tip The Wild Futures Monkey Sanctuary, just 1.5 miles away, looks after a range of monkeys including capuchins, marmosets, long-tailed macaques and woolly monkeys.

84 Lost Gardens of Heligan

Shhhhhhh! Don't wake her – or is it just a dream?

Heligan Garden has a wild romance about it in its snaking paths, hidden corners and steep valleys. At the heart of the garden is a slumbering figure amongst the trees and undergrowth – rather unromantically called the Mud Maid. She sleeps while her hair turns to grass and ivy weaves into her clothes. Are the lost gardens her dreamworld – who or what will waken her?

It's hard to see how 200 acres of garden could be lost, but these 200-year-old gardens were discovered by chance by Sir Tim Smit of Eden biome fame as an overgrown wilderness 30 years ago; they have been painstakingly restored to a small world of their own. At its centre is a well-ordered kitchen garden producing vegetables and fruit – including pineapples (ask to see the special growing methods their custodian uses to nurse them along). You can take a stroll through fruit tree tunnels and admire show-case vegetable beds then head out to the wilder valley and woodlands. Look out for the Giant's Head and the Grey Lady along the woodland walk – and explore jungle plantings; try the rope bridge crossing a valley (don't mind the wobble and the drop below, it's totally safe); look out for beavers; inspect the formal gardens; and get acquainted with the rare breeds of livestock (Tamworth pigs, Highland cows and Shire horses) that Heligan is stewarding.

When the winter festive season comes, around Mud Maid and a whole other world of giant mushrooms, flowers and creatures of the night are gently illuminated between light-festooned trees and giant ferns during the dark hours for the Heligan Night Garden. These magical evenings give the gardens a dreamlike quality – if you loved Disney's *Fantasia* you will love this. There is usually something new to see on a return visit and there is also cake – very good cake – which always adds that extra something to an experience. Plan to spend the whole day here, especially if there are children with you.

Address Pentewan, St Austell, PL26 6EN, www.heligan.com | Getting there By car, take the B 3273 from St Austell towards Mevagissey and follow the signs; bus 24 (First Kernow) or 23 (Go Bus Cornwall) from Mevagissey to St Austell, to Heligan car park | Hours Daily 10am – 5pm; last entry 3.30pm | Tip The Eden Project, where the famous biomes were constructed in a disused clay pit, is only half-an-hour's drive from Heligan.

85 Roche Rock
Be careful how you ascend

The village of Roche is named after the 65-foot-high rock that stands as a proud landmark dominating the landscape. 'Riche' is an old French-Norman word for rock, but the traditions here are Cornish.

Almost everywhere in Cornwall has a myth associated with it and Roche Rock does not miss out. This is another place where Jan Tregeagle, according to legend the most evil man in Cornwall, met his comeuppance after his pact with the Devil, getting his head stuck in the east window of the chapel perched at the top of the rock, with his body dangling outside. He was rescued by a priest who could not stand his constant screaming. (We meet him again near Helston, where legend has it that he tripped whilst carrying a sack full of sand, which blocked the river Cober and created Loe Bar.)

The chapel at the top was built in the 15th century and dedicated to St Michael the Archangel. It was used as shelter by a local hermit and is sometimes called the Roche Rock Hermitage. Earlier, in medieval times, the story goes that it was lived in by the father of the Tregarnick family, who isolated himself there having contracted leprosy. It must have been a safe place to live, as access is by steep steps cut into the stone, slippery when wet.

Nowadays you can climb an iron ladder to the chapel and look around inside, but be careful, it's a long way up and a long way down again! There are steep rocky sides to Roche Rock and you may come across rock climbers with their ropes – Roche Rock is listed on the British Mountaineering Council website as a midgrade climb, on schorl rock (composed of quartz and tourmaline), which gives good purchase for climbing. Don't try to climb unless you're an expert. Get to the top and there are fantastic views to the east and south across the china clay mining landscape, with the huge disused Goonbarrow works dominating the natural high point of Hensbarrow Downs.

Address Near the Cricket Club, Roche, PL26 8HB, www.what3words.com/ shifters.servers.loses | Getting there By car, take the A30 through Roche village, up the hill and first left past the Rock Inn; limited parking by the side of the road | Hours Unrestricted | Tip Goss Moor National Nature Reserve, 1.25 miles to the east, is an extensive landscape of heathland and wet woodland grown over an old tin-streaming site, with footpaths guiding you past the boggy areas.

86__ Treffry Viaduct
Water 90 feet up

As you drive north along the lovely wooded Luxulyan valley you will suddenly and unexpectedly see this gigantic Scheduled Ancient Monument towering 90 feet above you. There are 29 viaducts in Cornwall but this one is exceptional, being both viaduct (carrying a road or railway across a valley) and aqueduct (carrying water). The viaduct was built between 1839 and 1842 by Joseph Treffry, who was born Joseph Austen but changed his name by deed poll to Treffry when he inherited the Treffry family estate at Place House in Fowey (pronounced to rhyme with joy).

Treffry wanted to link his new harbour at Par on the south coast (strangely, built against the advice of Isambard Brunel) to the harbour at Newquay in the north, an engineering project that would provide water to his lucrative copper mine at Fowey Consols. The railway was actually a tramway, with wagons pulled by mules and horses; the rails were removed in the 1940s. The water channel, fed by a leat, which can still be seen but which no longer carries water due to leaks and erosion, was lined with puddled clay to keep it watertight and then covered with stone slabs – an amazing piece of engineering.

The water in the leat also powered a large 32-foot water wheel, which was used to haul wagons by cable up the 109-yard Carmears Incline through Carmears Wood. This carried the building stone for the viaduct and minerals from Fowey Consols. You can still see the building here although the water wheel has long gone. The viaduct is now owned by Cornwall Heritage Trust, who bought the viaduct from the Treffry family in 1989. There are plans to rewater the leats here, but not across the viaduct, as it leaks. The leats provide a useful resource for water-powered turbines and electricity generation – another, more modern, example of industrial activity within this beautiful wooded valley.

Address Par, PL24 2SU, www.what3words.com/routs.overhaul.indicate | **Getting there** The minor road between St Blazey and Luxulyan runs under the viaduct (park on the roadside), and you can walk up the valley side to the viaduct top | **Hours** Accessible 24 hours | **Tip** There are lots of walks to enjoy in Luxulyan Valley, including two circular walks – Luxulyan Valley Circular (3.4 miles) and Luxulyan Valley to Prideaux (4.9 miles); an app is available from www.iwalkcornwall.co.uk.

87 Trevethy Quoit

Our quoit is bigger than yours

For a serious archaeologist, or just a fan of the Flintstones, the less developed areas of Cornwall can be very exciting, with remains of Cornish history from the Stone Age to the last century scattered just about everywhere. As late Stone Age (known as Neolithic) tombs go – and Cornwall has more than its fair share – Trevethy Quoit is particularly impressive because of its height: it is the tallest in Cornwall, and has an enormous (and very heavy) granite capstone; it is known locally as the Giant's House.

The structure would have been even bigger when it was in use because the stones that now stand so dramatically against the Cornish sky, exposed to the battering weather, would have been capped, almost certainly with soil. Inside it is thought there would have been two 'rooms' where ceremonies to keep good relations with the natural world took place.

You are free to investigate the stone structure; as you move between the stones you get a sense of the importance of the structure for those who used it. A curious feature is the hole in the corner of the capstone – what its purpose was is anybody's guess, but creating that hole in granite would have taken real skill with just the stone and bone tools they were using.

A different landscape would have existed when the quoit was built; it wouldn't have been the enclosed field you see now – that probably dates back only 100 years or so. It's thought that Cornwall wasn't colonised by man until the late Stone Age and that the moorlands were settled first – there would not have been too many trees to clear, and there was plenty of stone to work with! Those early Cornishmen would have been skilled in moving and shaping the granite boulders that natural forces had strewn around the landscape, and it is at least partly due to the toughness of the stone that Cornwall has so many of these Stone Age remains to investigate.

Address Off the B 3254, Nr Darite, St Cleer, PL14 5JY, www.what3words.com/
scorch.muted.slimy | **Getting there** The Quoit is signposted off the minor road between
Darite and Tremar, just east of St Cleer on the south-eastern edge of Bodmin Moor | **Hours**
Unrestricted | **Tip** The Grade I-listed St Cleer Holy Well and Cross, only 0.6 miles away in
the centre of St Cleer; they date from the early 16th century and are very well preserved.

88 Gwennap Pit
Hear a whisper

From the air, this pit forms a perfect circle 120 feet across, with 11 rings leading down to a flat circular space in the centre, partly obscured by trees on the south-west side. This is not a mystical sign to the gods of a primitive people, or a landing place for aliens, but the site of a mining pit that collapsed into some of the tunnels that criss-cross the area around St Day, once the richest and most famous copper mining centre in the world. Even in the heavy Cornish rain it is said that the centre of the circle never floods, so there must be drainage from the lowest point into the mining adits below.

In 1762, the Methodist preacher John Wesley used the pit to preach to his congregation, spread out below him; at that time the pit was just a rough hollow but large enough to hold thousands of people. Wesley was the leader of the Methodists (so called because of their emphasis on methodical study) and as an itinerant preacher travelled throughout Cornwall and elsewhere, preaching at Gwennap Pit no fewer than 18 times. The extended, spread-out, rural-based population of Cornwall suited his practice of preaching outdoors; his outdoor congregations did not have to travel a long way to church and could freely come and go. It was less formal than the church and everyone was more equal, which suited the independent Cornish folk.

Sometime between 1803 and 1806 (well after John Wesley had died), local miners built 12 circular terraces still visible today. Here you can now sit and listen to the services still held here in the summer, or visit at your leisure and admire the surprising symmetry of the site. Does the bottom really not fill with water in heavy rain? It is said that the acoustics are marvellous so why not stand in the bottom, whisper a message and see if someone in the top row can hear you.

Address Busveal, Redruth, TR16 5HH | Getting there Signposted from the roundabout on the A393 Redruth and from the St Day road just west of Vogue | Hours Pit accessible 24 hours; visitor centre open in summer Mon–Fri 10am–4.30pm, Sat 10am–1pm, Sun from 3pm during services | Tip Less than a mile away is the Star Inn at Vogue pub. In 2022, the owners of the famous fashion magazine threatened to sue this village pub for using 'their' name. In fact, the pub is over 200 years old whereas the magazine was founded in 1916. *Vogue* magazine withdrew their threat and the owner of the Star Inn gave *them* permission to use the 'Vogue' name.

89 Alfrcd Wallis
Climbing the stairs to heaven

On a windswept hilltop above Porthmeor Beach you will find Barnoon Cemetery, from where you can gaze out on the Atlantic Ocean. Amongst the many graves, which include victims of shipwrecks and the *Titanic*, there is the wondrously unique tomb of the St Ives artist Alfred Wallis, a place of pilgrimage to lovers of art.

Alfred painted simple pictures on odd pieces of cardboard – of ships and seas and lighthouses, with no sense of perspective, each object on its own within the sea or sky, using household paint. He had begun his working life as a seaman on a schooner crossing the Bay of Biscay. At the age of 18 he was making voyages from Penzance to Newfoundland, but he later settled in St Ives. Here he married Susan, a much older woman who already had children, and worked first as a coastal fisherman, later running a marine stores business from where he sold ice cream. In 1922, after Susan's death, living on his own, and at the age of 70, he began painting to fill the lonely hours. He was 'discovered' by artists Ben Nicholson and Christopher Wood and gained some kind of fame, but thought his neighbours in Back Road West were jealous of him. You can stay in his cottage for a holiday – you do not have to be a primitive painter to do so.

Alfred knew the sculptor Barbara Hepworth, but she refused to design his headstone when he died. So it was Bernard Leach of the famous Leach Pottery who, after Wallis' death on 29 August, 1942, created the ceramic tiles which so beautifully adorn the tomb. The tiles show the small figure of Alfred Wallis entering a golden lighthouse on his long journey up the stairs to his God. Although he was held in esteem by artistic friends he made little money from his work and died almost penniless, save for a little money for his funeral. His paintings nowadays are scattered across the globe and sell for thousands of pounds.

Address Clodgy View, St Ives, TR26 1JG | **Getting there** In winter park in the Barnoon long-stay car park; in summer park in Trenwith car park and catch the shuttle bus to the town centre | **Hours** Accessible 24 hours | **Tip** The Tate Gallery is immediately next to the cemetery, with changing exhibitions and a café on the top floor with spectacular views over the Atlantic Ocean.

90 Barbara Hepworth Museum

Bronze sculpture in the garden

A tiny museum has been created out of the home where Barbara Hepworth lived and worked from 1949 until her death in 1975, in a fire that was probably caused by a lit cigarette when she fell asleep. Downstairs is an exhibition that shows aspects of her life, but climb the narrow staircase to the indoor gallery and go outside to her studio and you can see the tools and materials that she used to create her art. Best of all, you can sit here in her quiet garden sheltered from the westerly Cornish winds, above the bustle of the narrow streets, surrounded by shrubs, trees, bamboo and a tall solitary Chusan palm, and gaze at her bronze sculptures as the light changes, sunshine giving yellow lights and rain throwing watery patterns, with changing reflections at different times of day.

Barbara particularly loved the garden at night when the moonlight gave a new dimension to everything. Her sculptures are not of people or things but abstract shapes, powerful in their size, some with holes through which you can see the inside of the sculpture, with light shining through from the framed view behind, some with tensioned strings to connect the inner and outer surfaces and express the tension between the artist and the sea, the wind or the Cornish hills.

Hepworth said of her work: 'The forms which have had special meaning for me since childhood have been the standing form (which is the translation of my feeling towards the human being standing in landscape); the two forms (which is the tender relationship of one living thing beside another); and the closed form, such as the oval, spherical or pierced form (sometimes incorporating colour) which translates for me the association of meaning of gesture in landscape; in the repose of say a mother & child, or the feeling of the embrace of living things, either in nature or in the human spirit.'

Address Barnoon Hill, St Ives, TR26 1AD, www.tate.org.uk/visit/tate-st-ives/barbara-hepworth-museum-and-sculpture-garden | Getting there In winter park in the Barnoon long-stay car park; in summer park in Trenwith car park and catch the shuttle bus to the town centre | Hours Check the website for details | Tip At 38 feet high, the *Earth Goddess* at St Austell is the tallest ceramic sculpture in the United Kingdom. When it was unveiled in 2022, local opinion was mixed.

91 St Ives Bay Railway

The most scenic line in Britain?

Take this delightful train ride away from the Penzance to Paddington line at St Erth Park and Ride, and almost straightaway you are passing along the very edge of St Ives Bay, away from the cars, with one of the best views of this northern coast bay there is. The pity is that it only takes just over 10 minutes to cover its 4.25 miles, but it is much the best way to visit St Ives if you want a more relaxed expedition than by car and the feeling of being on holiday, even if you're local.

Opened in 1877, the line served the fishing industry of St Ives, transporting pilchards 'upcountry' through the station at St Erth. Then, as the fishing declined, and more and more people travelled by car, the line was marked for closure in the drastic Beeching cuts as part of the restructuring of the nationalised railway system in Great Britain in the 1960s. Luckily for St Ives it was saved by the then Minister for Transport, Barbara Castle, and it is now one of the best scenic lines in the country. The line was the last broad gauge passenger railway to be built in Britain but trains have been standard gauge since 1892.

The little train meanders along the coastal cliffs on a single line with the beaches, the harbour, the dunes and the estuary stretched out below for much of the way. If the tide has receded into the bay you can test your bird-watching skills on the many birds that use the extensive sand and mudflats for feeding and resting. There is a brief stop inland at the tiny Carbis Bay station, then down onto the open cliffs again from where, on one of the sparkling clear days so characteristic of this coast, you'll be able to see Godrevy Island with its lighthouse in the distance. When the train arrives in St Ives at Porthminster it's a short but steep walk down to the sandy beach with its notable café and promenade, or you can walk up the slope to St Ives' narrow streets.

Address St Erth station, Hayle, TR27 6JW; St Ives station, TR26 2GB, www.greatscenicrailways.co.uk/stations/st-erth-park-and-ride | Getting there St Erth station park and ride is easy to find on the road between Hayle and Penzance | Hours Train runs daily, all year round; check website for timetable | Tip Another coastal scenic railway in Cornwall is the Looe Valley line, which runs from the ancient town of Liskeard through wooded valley and along the edge of the saltmarsh in the Looe estuary.

92 The Crowns Engine Houses

Lost in a card game in TV's Poldark

It's great to feel the full force of the Atlantic as waves crunch onto the sea cliffs at Botallack, the wind sweeps up the slopes and salt spray stings your face. But look to the lower cliff and you see an iconic scene – the Crowns engine houses standing defiant against this endless battering.

In TV land, Ross Poldark knew the Crown Mine in its working days in the late 1780s; he had returned to his Cornish homeland from the American War of Independence to find his inheritance gone, the family tin and copper mine closed and his beloved Elizabeth married to his cousin Francis. In the *Poldark* novels by Winston Graham it was Francis who owned this mine, called Wheal Grambler. Under Francis the mine failed and was closed down and then he lost it in a card game to Ross's great rival George Warleggan. In fact, this mine didn't open until 1815 (when Ross would have been 45 years old) but it makes a dramatic backdrop to the film series. It is also a long way from the film location for Nampara, the Poldark home, an ancient granite manor house on the fringes of Bodmin Moor.

Mining was a boom and bust business, dependant on the price of copper and tin, and finding an easily worked mineral load. It was also dangerous. Below these engine houses runs a diagonal mine shaft running over 985 feet under the Atlantic Ocean; Crown Mine closed in 1895 when it flooded and the tin price crashed, though it re-opened in 1905 and closed finally in 1914. In the *Poldark* stories Graham commemorates eight men and a boy who lost their lives when a haul chain broke in 1863, in a fictional disaster caused by working without roof support at Wheal Grace (also filmed here).

Even then these cliffs would have been a haven for wildlife; six-spot burnet moths and silver-studded blue butterflies would have watched Elizabeth and Francis looking down at the mine buildings as they rued the loss of their mine.

Address Botallack, St Just, Penzance, TR19 7QQ | **Getting there** By car, take the B 3306 to car park at Botallack; bus 18 between Penzance and St Ives passes the entrance to the village, from which it is just over 0.5 mile's walk to the mine | **Hours** Unrestricted | **Tip** West Wheal Owles is just 440 yards south as the chough flies; this is the setting for the fictional Wheal Leisure owned by Ross Poldark.

93 Kurt Jackson Foundation

*Best Art Gallery in Cornwall in the Muddy
Stilettos Awards*

If you want to see huge landscapes of dramatic seas, sparkling rivers, glistening mudflats, brooding trees and estuary nightscapes all painted *en plein air*, then this is the place to come. Kurt Jackson understands the complexity of the natural world, focussing on its ever-changing light and emphasising the fragility of our wild places.

Still dynamic in his early sixties, painting in warm summers and with frozen fingers in winter, his energy is reflected in the paintings, drawings and sculptures; not the static images of many modern artists, but alive with light, colour and movement. There are regularly changing themed exhibitions, such as on the river Fowey in Cornwall which runs as a dark corridor from the higher reaches of Bodmin Moor down to the estuary where the Bodinnick Ferry crosses. He says 'rivers carry our memories, feelings and histories … and have a life of their own and support more life and lives than we could ever imagine.'

As an environmental campaigner, Jackson has supported a range of organisations, including Survival International and Friends of the Earth. He has been the artist in residence for Greenpeace, the Eden Project and Glastonbury Festival. Upstairs in the gallery there is space for collaborative exhibitions with charities including Surfers Against Sewage and the Royal National Lifeboat Institution. Kurt supported the RNLI by donating one of his paintings as a prize.

Depending on when you visit, you might see tiny pictures of Greenpeace against whaling ships, rock stars at Glastonbury Festival and RNLI lifeboats surging though spume-covered waves. All paintings are for sale, along with prints and themed books centred on his different exhibitions. You can get in free, safe in the knowledge that this is a green-built, sustainably managed carbon-negative gallery, powered by high-efficiency solar panels and ground-source heat pumps.

Address Jackson Foundation Gallery, North Row, St Just, TR19 7LB,
www.jacksonfoundationgallery.com | Getting there Park in the free car park in Lafrowda
Close, TR19 7JA, and follow the signs from the town square | Hours Generally open
Tue – Sat (closed for lunch), but check website for details | Tip Lafrowda Day is held on the
third Saturday of July every year as a celebration of community arts with live music, stalls
and community parades with withy sculptures and a torchlit procession.

94 An Gof
A name perpetual

In 1497, the Cornish rebelled against King Henry VII who was taxing Cornish people to help pay for his war against Scotland. The rebellion was led by Michael Joseph, called Michael An Gof ('Michael the blacksmith'), a St Keverne lad. In June that year he led his followers of Cornishmen across Cornwall protesting at the taxes. At Bodmin he was joined by Thomas Flamank, a lawyer, who claimed that the taxes were illegal: why should the Cornish people pay for protecting the border with Scotland, hundreds of miles away?

It is said that 6,000 men assembled at Bodmin, and that by the time they reached the border with Devon the army had grown to 15,000, with more people joining on the route. They marched on London, assembling at Blackheath on the side of the river Thames. Here their army was defeated at the Battle of Deptford Bridge on 17 June, 1497. An Gof and Flamank were hanged. This was the First Cornish Rebellion; a second, perhaps better known, was led later in the same year by Perkin Warbeck, a pretender to the English throne, but that too failed. A statue to An Gof and Flamank stands proudly at the entrance to St Keverne and a memorial dedicated to them can be seen on the church wall in St Keverne Square.

An Gof has since then had 'a name perpetual and a fame permanent and immortal', a symbol of Cornish identity and independence. Every year on 27th June, the anniversary of An Gof's death, a ceremony to honour his memory is held at St Keverne. Five hundred years after the rebellion, people from Cornwall – from children to grandmothers – under the name Keskerdh Kernow gathered together at St Keverne and marched the 330 miles to Blackheath, following the same route, sleeping in village halls on the way; this time the march was peaceful, a celebration of Cornish identity and uniqueness, with flags held high. An Early Day Motion in the House of Commons celebrating the march was tabled on 17 June, 1997 and signed by 33 MPs.

Address St Keverne, TR12 6PB | Getting there By car, drive into St Keverne on the B 3293 from Helston and the statues are on your left as you drive into the village | Hours Unrestricted | Tip The fishing village of Porthoustock (pronounced Prow'stock) is just a mile away. It has a pebble beach and is close to the Manacles, a popular spot for diving.

95   Roskilly's
Proper Cornish – cream on top

Forget the newbie rewilding projects, Roskilly's is a brilliant place where Joe Roskilly's vision for a wildlife-friendly farm has matured into just that. Best of all you can taste the produce. Joe started his 'rewilding' in this quiet corner of Cornwall by creating a nature trail round some ponds on his farm with advice from local wildlife experts. This was way back in the 1970s and the farm appeared in one of the very first editions of BBC's *Countryfile* with John Craven over 30 years ago, when Joe's ideas were far from mainstream. The importance of wildlife on the farm was taken seriously and the film even included an expert entomologist looking at the insect life of the Cornish hedgerows.

So this is one of the first organic farms in Britain and it continues to be a small working organic farm, at 20 acres or so, which is home to an all-important herd of ridiculously photogenic Jersey cows. You can watch them as they are milked and get to see some of the wilder areas of the farm, including those ponds, on the mile-long walk.

Perhaps the real highlight, though, is the ice cream, the best there is, made from the farm's own Jersey herd milk. There are all kinds of flavours including one offs such as the Coronation ice-cream in 2023, with streaks of raspberry, vanilla and blueberry. In the Croust House restaurant ('croust' is Cornish for a snack), you can have a cream tea the Cornish way, with cream on top of the jam with your scone. Then you can follow the map on the interpretation boards and stroll down the lane through the Old Withy Woods and around the ponds, catching sight of the wide blue ocean and open sea-cliffs on your way.

The small courtyard at the Croust house is the place to sit on a sunny summer's day, but in winter you can warm yourself inside near the log fire. The courtyard is a venue for free musical events on summer evenings, when the restaurant offers an evening menu.

Roskilly's

Address Tregellast Barton Farm, St Keverne, TR12 6NX, www.roskillys.co.uk | Getting there Heading south on the B 3293 past Goonhilly Satellite dishes and after two miles turn right onto the B 3294 to Coverack; after 328 yards, turn left following the signs to Roskilly's | Hours Daily 9am–8pm | Tip Halzephron Herb Farm has new premises on Tregellast Farm, the home of Roskillys, after moving from Halzephron (aka 'The Cliffs of Hell' in Cornish!) near Gunwalloe; their one local outlet is in the Roskilly's shop, where you can buy their handmade sauces, jams and pickles.

96__Japanese Garden
Mossy green islands on gravel seas

The tranquillity in this single-acre garden in the sheltered Vale of Lanherne is what makes this a Cornish gem. At its heart are the essential items of the Japanese garden philosophy – peaceful contemplation, an emphasis on the beauty and meaning of natural features, and the art of miniaturisation.

But the design can be appreciated at whichever level you choose. Taken at face value, it is a lovely garden full of interesting plants, paths and quiet corners where you can sit, relax and note inspiring design ideas to take away with you. Yet all the elements of the Japanese philosophy are there to investigate and consider. You enter through a traditional Torii gate and wind your way along paths, over bridges, past the Koi pond, waterfalls, shrines and the Teahouse, all features with Japanese symbology but with reference to the pre-existing place, including a dilapidated barn incorporated into the Teahouse.

The Buddhist tradition is maintained in the Zen Garden, where gravel carefully raked anew each day surrounds the miniature islands of mossy mountains. This makes a tiny but entire landscape that can be peacefully enjoyed from the shelter of the adjacent timber pavilion with the rustling of the bamboo and the song from the wind chimes and birds completing the peaceful atmosphere.

The garden opened in 1997 after six years of development alongside a bonsai nursery. A careful approach, in tune with its philosophy, has brought its rewards, and the garden continues to evolve whilst keeping its unique Cornish character, drawing on the surrounding valley landscape and woodland and using local slates and granites. In autumn there is an explosion of colour as the many maples burst into their fiery autumn colours, and in spring cherries and azaleas brighten the garden. It's a place that can be returned to time and again, in all weathers, over the seasons and with passing years.

Address St Mawgan, near Newquay, TR8 4ET, www.japanesegarden.co.uk | **Getting there** Easy to find at the bottom of the hill in the tiny village of St Mawgan | **Hours** Mar–Nov; check the website for details | **Tip** There is a small Japanese Garden set within the extensive 30-acre Pinetum Garden at Holmbush Road, Holmbush, St Austell, PL25 3RQ (www.pinetumgardens.com), worth visiting for its large plant collection and champion trees.

97 King Arthur's Great Halls
Our once and future king

Think of Tintagel and you think of King Arthur, the legendary British king who fought against the invading Anglo Saxons in the 5th century, the man who pulled the sword Excalibur from the stone, who created the Round Table where no one could sit at the head and everyone was equal, who loved Guinevere and was advised by Merlin the magician. If his life ended at Loe Bar, it is said it began here at Tintagel Castle, set on the island beyond the headland.

You can visit the 13th-century castle across the new bridge, walk amongst its remains on the steep cliffs and climb to the other-worldly Gallos statue on the top. But if you want something with easy access and a colourful interpretation of the legend, take a look at the Grade II-listed Great Halls, opened by Frederick Thomas Glasscock in 1933. He was fascinated by the Arthurian legend and founded the Order of the Fellowship of the Knights of the Round Table in 1927 (wound up when he died in 1934 but revived in 1993) based on the symbolism and ideals of the Arthurian and Christian traditions. The centrepiece of the Great Halls is a long, rectangular hall known as the Hall of Chivalry, with the 8-foot granite Round Table at one end and a model of King Arthur's throne at the other.

The highlights here, however, are the 73 stained-glass windows designed and constructed by Veronica Whall from 1930–33. She was a well-known stained-glass artist, with many of her works in New Zealand. Her motto was 'The three things technically essential to the making of a stained glass window are glass, lead and light… for lead is our medium, and light is our colour.' The windows depict each Knight of the Round Table with his shield; other windows depict some of the virtues the knights promised to keep. These windows are probably the largest collection of stained-glass panels of King Arthur created in the 20th century.

Address Fore Street, Tintagel, PL34 0DA, www.kingarthursgreathalls.co.uk | Getting there There are plenty of car parks in Tintagel | Hours Mar–Oct Tue–Sun 10am–5pm | Tip The National Trust-owned Old Post Office, also on Fore Street, is an atmospheric 14th-century yeoman's farmhouse with a famously wavy slate roof and 600 years of history.

98__Cremyll Ferry
Cross the Tamar into Devon

The remote south eastern corner of Cornwall is one that often gets passed by since the building of the Tamar Bridge, but it is so much more than just the edge of the Duchy. At the end of the road approach to Cremyll village there is a spectacular view from this quiet shore, looking across the Hamoaze section of the Tamar to the big waterfront of Plymouth on the Devon shore. The Cremyll Foot Ferry runs from the quay and you can hop on – it usually runs every half an hour – and be in Plymouth in minutes. You arrive at Admiral's Hard on the Stonehouse Peninsula of Plymouth after passing the impressive buildings of the Royal William Yard, recently repurposed as a chic residential complex. But that is in Devon, so no more of that.

The ferry crossing is at a narrow point where the currents on the tidal river are fast, hence the name given to the promontory on the opposite shore – Devil's Point. Modern power makes light work of the currents but this is an ancient foot ferry that is believed to have been used in Saxon times and first recorded in 1204, so for much of its history it has been a rowed crossing. At the start of the 1900s the ferry towed a 'Horseboat' which could carry two-wheeled carts and horses or the carriage for the Earl of the nearby estate. You can see a hand winch near the Cremyll toll office, which was used to drag the Horseboat up over the beach. The last Horseboat was probably lost in the 1940s and by then the Torpoint Ferry offered a safer crossing for larger traffic.

There are times when the harbour master declares the waters closed to the ferry to allow for shipping, including naval movements, so the ferry has to wait but you get the chance to see ships coming and going between Cremyll and Devil's Point. In mid August Cremyll is a great place to watch the British Firework Championships without having to cross into Devon!

Address Quay Cremyll, Cremyll, Torpoint, PL10 1HX, www.plymouthboattrips.co.uk | Getting there By car, drive to the end of the B 3247 | Hours Every 30 minutes from morning to evening, depending on the tide; reduced hours in winter | Tip Mount Edgcumbe Park, the home of the Earl of Mount Edgcumbe, is just next door to Cremyll and open to the public; there are extensive parklands, a listed house and a charming orangery and café to visit.

99 Cornwall's Dark Skies
Observatory for Cornwall

Cornwall has been identified as the fourth darkest county in England because of the large areas of countryside without street, housing or industrial lighting and its long coastline with dark sea beyond.

There are two official dark sky regions in Cornwall: Bodmin Moor, a huge area of largely open-access land designated as a Dark Sky Park in 2017, and West Penwith – designated as an International Dark Sky Park in 2021 – where 6,000 years ago Neolithic people built stone structures pointing to the heavenly constellations. This is where you too can walk across the moors looking up at the stars and there is even a dedicated stargazing walk to the top of Chapel Carn Brea, just inland from Cape Cornwall in the far west (take a torch and wrap up warm). Look out to sea and you might just see the phosphorescence of the waves as they crash against the shore. On cloudy nights you will see how our artificial lighting creates unwelcome 'sky glow' as it is reflected back down from the clouds.

Away from the conurbations, on clear nights, the dark skies of Cornwall are great for exploration. So if you go outside, turn off your mobile phone and wait till your eyes have become accustomed to the dark, you will be able to see the moon, some of the planets, constellations and the Milky Way. You might even see some wildlife – 60% of wildlife in the world is nocturnal.

To take a closer look at the night sky you can visit the Observatory for Cornwall, on a dark hilltop in mid-Cornwall, where the efforts of an energetic group of volunteers have resulted in a growing community astronomical facility, with two purpose built 20-foot night sky observation domes, eight refractor and reflector telescopes, a library and study hut. The charity that runs the site invites anyone interested, be they juniors, seniors, students or amateurs, to join them in using the equipment for star and planet gazing, deep astronomical investigations and the chance to make new discoveries.

Address Northdowns Wheal Busy, near Chacewater, Truro, TR1 4NZ,
www.observatoryforcornwall.co.uk | Getting there By car from Chacewater, drive west up
the hill and take the first right at the crossroads then right again on an unmarked road past
old mining buildings; the Observatory is at the end of the track | Hours Check by emailing
info@observatoryforcornwall.co.uk | Tip Why not visit some of Cornwall's famous coastal
destinations at night, when the scenery is all about the sky? At St Agnes Head you can even
see glow-worms shining green against the heathland.

100_ *The Drummer*
A naked man!

This statue, standing where once there was a quay, has a compelling message: known as *The Drummer*, he portrays strength and resilience, characteristics of the Cornish people. Here the drum beats a different time to places outside Cornwall. He balances on a ball, which represents the earth's globe across which many Cornish folk travelled to work in distant mines and it is said that 'at the bottom of every hole is a Cornishman'.

This 15-foot bronze statue of a man banging a drum had to be naked, according to Tim Shaw, the sculptor, because if you put clothes on him it would belong to a particular time and not be a universal figure. If you dressed him in jeans, the statue would belong to now and not be relevant to the past. So it is timeless, like a Greek statue, and hardly controversial; it's just unusual that it's a naked man and not a naked woman. It is meant to be timeless, like Cornwall itself. It's meant to represent Cornwall, and it's made of an ingot of Cornish tin and an ingot of Cornish copper.

Look carefully on the side of the drum and you can see a stylised image of a lamb and flag. Ingots of metal in Cornwall have been stamped with distinctive marks since the early 18th century, representing particular smelting houses, and the lamb carrying a flag has been used since 1715 – especially for ingots sent to Catholic countries (giving the ingot a slightly religious context).

The Drummer looks as though he is unbalanced, about to fall off the globe, which looks as though it will roll forward towards the river. This gives a great energy to the work. There are circles marked into the ground of the Lemon Quay here and these represent the rings that radiate out from a pebble thrown into water. The apparently solid ground that *The Drummer* stands on is in fact covering several commercial quays, including Lemon Quay itself, that were part of a busy port on the Truro river.

Address Back Quay, Truro, TR1 2LL | Getting there Easily found in the centre of Truro in front of the Hall for Cornwall and near the bus station | Hours Unrestricted | Tip The main entrance for the Hall for Cornwall is just at *The Drummer*'s back; this newly refurbished performing arts theatre has an eclectic range of visiting shows throughout the year.

101 Joseph Antonio Emidy

Britain's first composer of the African diaspora

You only have to step past St Keyne Church's schoolroom lychgate to get an immediate sense of being in the presence of local history. Amongst the many headstones is one for Joseph Emidy, a man with a most unusual life story, a celebrated musician who had arrived in Falmouth on 28 February, 1799.

Joseph had been released from the British frigate *Indefatigable*, having been press-ganged and endured four years of entertaining the sailors with their hornpipes and jigs, rather than playing the classical music he had learnt at Lisbon opera. Remarkable enough you might think, but at 12 years old Joseph had been sold into slavery from his home in Guinea to work on plantations in Brazil, before he was taken to Portugal where his talent as a musician was spotted. It's not clear if he was a free man at this point but the frigate commander soon put a stop to that by having Joseph kidnapped.

Freedom came eventually when he was released at Falmouth at a time when slavery was disappearing in Britain. With local help he established himself as an admired violinist, composer and music teacher. He married local girl Jenefer Hutchins and they had eight children. He became a prominent musician in the southwest, Leader of Truro Philharmonic Orchestra and composer of works taken to London by the Cornish MP and student of Emidy, James Silk Buckingham.

Sadly, for the times, his ethnicity outweighed his musical genius; he was advised to remain outside London musical circles and his works have been completely lost, though his achievements are not forgotten. His arrival in Falmouth is now marked by a plaque outside Falmouth parish church, and a wooden plaque showing a violin and map of Africa resides in Truro Cathedral. Truro City Council decided a blue plaque on the façade of Truro Assembly Rooms, where he was known to perform, would spoil its appearance! Judge for yourself.

Inscription on headstone:

HERE LIE DEPOSITED
the mortal remains of
Mr Jos. Antonia Emidy
who departed this life.
on the 25th of April
1835
AGED 60 YEARS.
And sacred to whose memory
this tribute of affection is erected
by his surviving family.

He was a native of PORTUGAL,
which Country he quitted about
forty years since; and, pursuing the
Musical profession, resided in
Cornwall until the close of
his earthly career:

Devoted to thy soul inspiring strains
Sweet Music thee he hail'd his chief delight
...

Address 2 Knights Hill, Truro, TR1 3UY | **Getting there** At the church, walk past the lychgate along the lower path for 110 yards; the headstone is on the bank to your left under a large spreading yew tree | **Hours** Churchyard accessible 24 hours | **Tip** Penrose Water Gardens (Shortlanesend, Truro, TR4 9ES) has six acres of ponds, waterlilies, marshland and woodland, and is open daily 10am–4pm unless wet winter weather forces closure.

102 Piero's
Ciao!

Piero's Ristorante & Pizzeria is a little bit of the Mediterranean in the middle of Cornwall. It's a family business that's been serving authentic Italian food using fresh local ingredients for 25 years and is very much a part of Truro.

In Cornwall restaurants can come and go with the foodie fashions, but Piero's continues to offer a friendly Italian atmosphere and good menu for all ages, bambini and adulto alike. The décor is gently Italian with Venetian masks on the walls, gingham tablecloths and bright colours on the front, with an open fire / wood burner when the weather turns colder, so it's always cheering just arriving through the small courtyard, even on a wet Cornish evening. You may be greeted by Piero himself, or his Sardinian colleague Max, so a little Italian greeting always goes down well.

Be prepared for plenty of energetic Italian banter between the staff; you can even practise your evening class Italian when you are ordering, if you dare – they are used to it and might even help with pronunciation!

There are freshly made pizzas if that is your thing; you can watch them being made on the spot (try the Calzone, a stuffed and rolled pizza base, or Pizza Inferno, or design one yourself). Or go for one of their wide range of traditional dishes such as Petto di Pollo Sofia Loren, Saltimbocca alla Romana, Anatra al Pepe Verde, or one of their big range of pasta dishes such as Linguine Polpa di Granchio, as well as daily specials. There are Italian ice creams for dessert and, as you would expect, the wines are all Italian.

Booking your table by telephone is the best way to ensure a seat, and be sure to give yourself time if you need to get to the theatre because fast food is not the Italian way. They open for lunch and evening meals and they can get very busy. You'll love the informality and the friendliness. So – Buon Appetito!

Address Kenwyn Street, Truro, TR1 3DJ, www.pieros-pizzeria.co.uk | Getting there Easily found just off Victoria Square | Hours Open for lunch and dinner Mon–Sat | Tip At Boscawen Park on the south side of Truro you can play tennis, watch a game of cricket in the summer, see your children play in the playground, and stroll along the banks of the Truro river.

103— The Red Lion

You don't know what you've got till it's gone

Buildings come and go, and like many town centres in the 1960s there was a push to modernise Truro. The town was not exempt from drastic changes both planned and, maybe conveniently, unplanned. Looking down the width of Lemon Street from the top to the far end, you can see the modern façades of shops in Boscawen Street where the Red Lion Hotel once stood. It was a magnificent building, a much-loved hotel and restaurant with a long and important history in the city. Built as a family home in 1671, in 1770 it became the Red Lyon Inn and Tavern, known as one of the best places to stay in Truro with lodging rooms, billiard room, stabling and 'an excellent assortment of wines'. This may well be where Winston Graham imagined Ross Poldark stayed on his visits 'to town'.

The Red Lion stood here until 14 July, 1967, when a runaway lorry, brakes having failed, drove down Lemon Street, along its flat lower section, crossed Boscawen Street, veered right and headed straight into the front of the hotel where it came to rest, supporting much of the building frontage. Luckily, the lorry driver avoided serious injury.

It took only four weeks for the decision to be made to tear the building down, despite local concerns. A modern supermarket arose, resplendent in its bland concrete face and brutal architecture. But for many who knew Cornwall at that time, the memories of this distinguished building with its four floors and many rooms linger. There was a splendid 17th-century oak staircase (which mysteriously disappeared in the same year the building was destroyed), much oak furniture, an open-timbered ceiling in the chandelier-lit dining hall, and comfortable seating in the main lounge, behind full-length velvet curtains under a moulded ceiling.

Standing in the Co-op supermarket that occupies its space now, the loss to the city is only too obvious and is still spoken of by some with scepticism, suspicion, doubts and misgivings.

Address 26 Boscawen Street, Truro, TR1 2QQ | Getting there Easy to find in the centre of Truro | Hours Unrestricted from outside | Tip The façade of Truro Assembly Rooms can be found at Highcross, to the side of the west door of Truro Cathedral, which was built later. This was the centre of elegant Georgian social life in Truro, where many balls were held and plays and performances were produced.

104 Royal Cornwall Museum
From 6th-century stones to Lego

This historic museum was in danger of being closed in an act of cultural vandalism, due to proposed changes in the way Cornwall Council funds creative and cultural organisations. But it has survived – at least for now. Come while you can – every addition to visitor income helps.

Founded by the Royal Institution of Cornwall in 1818, the museum is housed in the former Truro Savings Bank building, erected in 1845. Walk past the Trewinnard Coach built in the 1750s, veer right to see the wildlife exhibition, then inspect the Rialton Stone. Dating back to the 6th century, the stone's Latin inscription reads *BONE-MIMORI (F)ILLI TRIBUNI*, which translates as 'In loving memory of (missing name) of a son of Tribunus'.

Nearby is the portrait of 'the Cornish giant', Anthony Payne (1612–1691), who stood 7 feet 4 inches tall and weighed 32 stone, and who took part in the Battle of Stamford Hill; you can stand in a model of his footprints. Next, walk up the impressive bifurcated staircase, past the Art Nouveau sculpture by Esther Mary Moore *At the Gates of the Past* – a woman consumed by thought, with poppies at her feet, symbolic of sleep; she would be an ideal companion for *The Drummer* who stands outside the Hall for Cornwall.

The first floor – from where you can look down at the displays below – houses a programme of changing exhibitions. You might see work by the Cornish artist Bryan Pearce – one of Cornwall's foremost naïve painters – or an innovative exhibition based on the five million pieces of Lego that were washed from a container ship in 1997 and ended up on Cornwall's shores, or perhaps an exhibition with a skewed and one-sided interpretation of Britain's colonial past. Who knows what you will see when you visit? On permanent display are items from the Egyptology and Geology collections; probably not on display are Winston Graham's typewriter – on which he wrote his *Poldark* stories – and cabinets of Cornish moths and butterflies.

Address River Street, Truro, TR1 2SJ, www.royalcornwallmuseum.org.uk | Getting there Easy to find in River Street | Hours Tue–Sat 10am–4pm; also Mon 10am–4pm during school holidays | Tip St Agnes Museum, Penwinnick Road, St Agnes, TR5 0PA (open Apr–Oct) is full of fascinating artefacts and information about St Agnes, especially relating to mining and maritime history – a real 'cabinet of curiosities'.

105 __ Truro Cathedral
The very first Christmas Nine Lessons and Carols

Truro Cathedral sits at the heart of the city, its three spires reaching up out of the main streets radiating around it. It is only 109 years old, an impressive honey-coloured Gothic Revival building that took nearly 30 years to complete, hindered by lack of funds but not determination.

The building is a mix of quirks and glories. Once inside there is plenty to admire including a life-size ebony-like Madonna and Child, stunning rose windows, a fine altar screen of Bath stone illustrating Christian stories (as well as a pre-Christian Green Man on the southern screen), and a fine Henry Willis organ. Look upwards to see a stunning high vaulted ceiling. Intriguingly, from the gallery – accessed by a narrow winding stone staircase built into the west end – you look along the nave and notice a bewildering bend in alignment that arose to avoid building into the street. Local stones were used – green Lizard serpentine in the font, local granites for strength, Duporth stone in the pillars. The architects were sufficiently pleased with the design to build a smaller version in Auckland, New Zealand. Within the building is the remaining south aisle of the 16th-century parish church of St Mary the Virgin, where the sun streams through stained-glass windows making the aisle gloriously colourful.

An important element that contributes to the cathedral's vibrancy is its musical life; its origin seems to flow from its first bishop, E. W. Benson (father of E. F. Benson, who wrote the *Mapp and Lucia* novels). Before completion of the cathedral, services were held in a wooden building, known as 'The Shed'. It was there, on Christmas Eve in 1880, that Bishop Benson introduced his service of Nine Lessons and Carols, supposedly to entice in the disorderly folk on Truro's streets. The idea caught on and the service evolved into the famous King's College Festival of Nine Lessons and Carols.

Address St Mary's Street, Truro, TR1 2AF, www.trurocathedral.org.uk | **Getting there** Unmissable in the centre of Truro | **Hours** Open to the public Mon–Sat 10am–5pm, Sun 11.30am–4pm | **Tip** Just inside the mouth of the Fal estuary is the tiny village of St Just in Roseland, its 13th-century church set beside a tidal creek. Sir John Betjeman thought the churchyard is perhaps the most beautiful on Earth, and the church is particularly worth a visit in December for its Festival of Light.

106 — Truro Leats
Victorian plumbing

Truro has an intriguing open-air Victorian feature on its streets that is generally ignored by passers-by in the inner city. The shallow channel in the granite on the street edge is part of a network that makes up the Truro leats, a system of open water channels believed to have been built into the city by the Victorians to manage the inevitable debris that went hand in hand with horse transport – mud, manure and urine.

Being built on the juncture of the rivers Allen and Kenwyn, there was no shortage of flowing water to maintain the Truro leats, but more recent flooding problems in the city have resulted in the removal of weirs on the upper system. Nevertheless, standing at High Cross outside the cathedral, a good deal of the remaining system can be seen nearby. If you walk through pedestrian lanes between buildings to the west you arrive at a back lane known as The Leats. There is no sign of them above ground here, but crossing Castle Street you find the Kenwyn River in a deep channel on the left and a wide feeder leat running on the upper channel to your right. Further along, below Victoria Gardens, the leat is still used to feed a fish pond and waterfalls via an old hydraulic ram pump, still visible near the river.

The leats are still opened when there is sufficient water in the Kenwyn River, subject to repair works, and then you will see clear water running down the side of Pydar and Bosacawen Streets, much to the delight of small children and thirsty dogs. Look out for the metal eyes sunk into the granite channels, which were probably used for tethering horses. Where the leat channels disappear under the pavements there is a maze of interconnecting leats that make their way to either the Lemon Quay or the New Bridge areas, where they reconnect to drop into the rivers. Nowadays the city council is proud and protective of this individual city feature and hopes to see it restored.

Address The Leats, Truro, TR1 3AG | Getting there Easily found behind Truro Museum | Hours Unrestricted | Tip Victoria Gardens is a small urban park full of trees, colourful flowering plant displays, and grassy slopes where you can relax, just a short walk from the city centre.

107 Walsingham Place
Homes for mistresses

Tucked away near the centre of Cornwall's capital city is Walsingham Place, an intriguing and charming corner of Truro. You may stumble into it accidentally as you hurry to get back to the ugly multistorey car park that towers over it, but once you've found it you will be drawn back to this small tranquil corner again.

The buildings along each side now house local businesses. but they have had a colourful history. Four hundred years ago you would have been standing on boggy ground on the banks of the river Kenwyn, which now flows in a narrow culvert behind the terrace. By the end of the 1600s, development had begun and this area was called Caribee Island – probably referring to the slave trade economy carried out in the port of Truro.

By the mid-18th century, with the abolition of the British slave trade, a Methodist chapel appeared on the site and a community of local businesses and residents developed so that by 1837, following the building of Lemon Street, the local MP, Mr Turner, and local businessman Mr Ferris were prompted to build Walsingham Place. The official history of Walsingham Place is that its residents were small businesses and local families, but an unofficial version tells the rather different story of how the local businessmen and gentry housed their mistresses here, the back doors allowing them to come and go unseen.

The Enys Estate has owned the land here since the early 18th century and would still own more except for a lapse in judgement by the Rev Enys in 1870, when he lost land in a card game – and we now have Mallets ironmongers in Victoria Square as a result! In 1964, Truro was undergoing radical changes, with large areas of housing being demolished. Doing away with Walsingham Place was on the list, but the Poet Laureate John Betjeman got wind of the plan. No one seems to know how he managed it, but after his campaigning Walsingham Place was saved.

Address Walsingham Place, Truro, TR1 2LP | Getting there Park in the Moorfield multi-storey car park at Calenick Street, Truro, TR1 2QD and Walsingham Place is immediately on the north-east side as you climb down the steps | Hours Accessible 24 hours | Tip Lemon Street is a short walk away. This is a fine old Georgian street with many Grade II-listed properties, and was named after the merchant William Lemon, who built houses in the street at the start of the 19th century. There was a plan at one time to build a new wide road across the middle, but luckily the plan was rejected.

108 The Bridge Over the Camel

The bridge built on wool

This bridge has a gruesome past – it is the bridge where the head of the Catholic priest Cuthbert Mayne was set upon a pole for all to see after he was hanged, drawn and quartered in Launceston in 1577 for supporting the Pope against Queen Elizabeth I. He was canonized in 1970 by Pope Paul VI. Also here, in 1646, Oliver Cromwell held the Bridge with 500 Dragoons and 1,000 horsemen but the opposing Royalist army withdrew without a fight. In 1845, George Wombwell's Travelling Menagerie got stuck on the bridge (it was too narrow); it's not certain which animals he exhibited here, but probably he had an elephant, an Indian rhino, llamas, panthers, leopards, hyenas, a kangaroo and his favourite animal – Nero the Lion. Cars didn't cross till 1901.

The town was originally called Wade, from the Old English 'waed' meaning a ford (fewer words are derived from Cornish the further towards England you go). The river here is tidal to Polbrook Bridge (two miles upstream) with a roughly 6.5-foot tidal range, so cross at low tide – but pray for a safe crossing before you go and give thanks afterwards if you reach the other side, as they did before the bridge was built. It was a dangerous crossing and several people and farm animals died, perhaps stuck in the mud as the tide came in.

The bridge was finally built in 1468, and was 650-feet long with 17 stone arches – and the town became Wadebridge. The story was that the bridge was built on sacks of wool, hence the name, but it is of course built on solid rock. Now widened but reduced in length, with 13 arches, it is a mere 426-feet long. Thirty years ago, holiday traffic used to get stuck on the bridge, as it carried the main A 39 trunk road, but in 1991 a new bridge (612-yards long) was built over the Camel and traffic now bypasses the town, leaving it a quiet, charming place for sightseeing and shopping.

Address Wadebridge, PL27 7DA | Getting there The bridge is in the centre of town | Hours Unrestricted | Tip The northern section of the Camel Trail starts from the edge of the town. You can walk, cycle (you can hire bikes) or ride your horse 5.5 miles along the disused railway line to Padstow, with glorious views of the river.

109 St Breock Downs

The old and the new

St Breock Downs, high on the hills above Wadebridge, at 656 feet above sea level, is an ideal situation for both ancient monuments and 21st-century wind turbines, the contrast of the old little and modern large. There are two ancient standing stones here: one, the St Breock Menhir, stands in a farmer's field with no public access but it's easy to see from the road; the other, known as the Longstone or Men Gurta (meaning the 'Stone of Waiting') stands amidst open heathy ground and is easily reached along a track. The larger of the two, standing at 10 feet tall, Longstone is the largest, heaviest monolith in Cornwall, weighing about 18.5 tons, and probably dating to the late Neolithic to mid-Bronze Age (around 2500–1500 B.C.). Stones and turbines were both placed by man, but the turbines tower over these ancient stones, standing tall with a maximum tip height of 328 feet and dating back to as long ago as 2015.

The Longstone used to stand 16 feet high but now is only just over 9.8 feet due to the marked lean to the north. It fell over in 1945 but was re-erected in 1956 after some archaeological investigations. By contrast, the wind turbines have become taller, with the 11 original turbines (with a blade diameter of 121 feet generating 450kW of power) being replaced by five turbines with a blade diameter of 263 feet each generating 2000kW of power.

The turbines are not popular with everyone but you cannot deny their majesty – and of course they harness the energy of the plentiful winds on these downs. The blades do make a whooshing noise and can cause harm to birds and bats; bats can suffer barotrauma but birds become accustomed to them, flying round rather than through the circling blades.

To build a wind farm you must go through a complicated planning process; it is probably safe to assume that in Neolithic times they would just have done what they wanted, with no red tape.

Address St Breock Downs, Rosenannon, PL30 5PN, www.what3words.com/
energy.goodness.tint | Getting there Access is on a minor road from Wadebridge to
Rosenannon. The Longstone is by a byroad on the west side at the hilltop; the Menhir can
be seen from the roadside here | Hours Accessible 24 hours | Tip The Royal Cornwall Show,
an annual three-day event, is held on the nearby Wadebridge showground in early June. One
of the few remaining traditional agricultural shows in the UK it brings together farming
folk, steam engines, farming machinery, keen gardeners, livestock of all shapes and sizes,
dogs, cats, bees and horses.

110__ The Trevanion Culverhouse

Just popping into the medieval supermarket

Tucked away on the edge of a modern housing estate on the outskirts of Wadebridge you will find a small circular building known as the Culvery – a well-maintained structure built by hand from the local slate stone in Norman times. The clue to this curious structure is the name: 'culvery' probably originates from the old Welsh word for dovecote, and a culver is a pigeon.

Here is the medieval equivalent of a supermarket. Inside you will see rows of slots in the stone-built walls where the pigeons would have nested. The building has been beautifully built, with a domed keystone-finished roof, the Norman style for such structures, inside which there would have been a moveable wooden frame and ladders giving access for tending the nests and birds on the higher levels. There are approximately 160 nest holes so that's a good store of potential food. It is not known what the official title was for the guy but he, or maybe she, would have been harvesting the eggs and 'squabs' (young domestic pigeons) for food for the lord of the manor.

The bird being 'farmed' was probably the domesticated pigeon known as the feral pigeon (*Columba livia domestica*), probably the world's oldest domesticated bird whose ancestor, the rock dove, now lives only on the remote sea cliffs and islands of Scotland and Northern Ireland.

Humans have probably been using pigeons as a food source in the Middle East for 10,000 years. The practice of housing them in dovecotes would have been introduced to Europe by the Romans during their years of Empire. It seems it was the privilege of the local lord, who would have had a ready supply of eggs and meat and may also have used the excrement for fertilizer.

The present-day neighbours would probably not welcome its being put back into operation – the smell would have been pretty unpleasant!

Address Trevanion Road, Trevanion, Wadebridge, PL27 7DX, www.what3words.com/blotches.activates.staples | Getting there By car, drive out of the centre of Wadebridge on Trevanion Road until you come to a turning into The Culvery on your left; follow this road into the housing estate, as far as the dead end, where the dovecote is ahead of you between two modern houses | Hours Accessible 24 hours | Tip Wadebridge Museum at Trebur House, Chapel Lane, PL27 7NJ, holds a large collection of photographs of the local district; entry is free.

111 The Mermaid of Zennor

Then I will go with ye – for with ye is where I belong

It comes as a bit of a surprise to find a mermaid in a village church, but the Mermaid of Zennor has an important role in the history of this small, ancient village. Legend has it that mermaids are generally bad news, especially for men who are lured to their doom beneath the waves by these enchanting creatures. And though, true to form, this mermaid stole away a human man, the local folk felt her important enough to have her carved figure in their church.

Two versions of the legend exist, but common to both is the church where young Matthey Trewella sang in the choir, and where either the visiting mermaid fell in love with his voice or Matthey fell in love with Morveren, the mysterious cloaked woman who visited when he sang. So it seems the young Matthey was fated to fall in love and disappear with this particular daughter of the sea god, never to be seen again, and the carving – on the very seat she sat in – is there to warn of the dangers of beautiful mermaids. The dark ornate seat is over 600 years old and the end is rather roughly carved, but you can clearly see the long flowing hair, the comb and mirror she is holding, and her fish tail.

But this tale doesn't end with Matthey's disappearance; there is a story of him still living under the waves below the cliffs of Pendour Cove with his mermaid and their children, and that they give warning to the fishermen of storms by singing deep and low, or telling of good weather by singing sweet and high. Sitting above the cove you may hear them singing, though this is not a beach for swimming.

Whatever the truth, the Mermaid of Zennor has inspired poetry, songs, plays and paintings from far and wide, even a movie and the name of the locally made ice cream. The Cornish folksinger Brenda Wootton sang 'Mermaid', a particularly ethereal mermaid's song, and the Cornish poet Charles Causely wrote of the Merrymaid of Zennor.

Address St Senara's Church, Zennor, TR26 3BY, www.zennorchurch.com | **Getting there** By car follow the B 3306 between St Ives and St Just, turn in to the village of Zennor, follow the side road, and the church is on the right | **Hours** Daily, approximately 9am – 6pm | **Tip** On a less romantic note you can see reminders of historic epidemics in the Plague Stones preserved in West Cornwall. The best example is in Zennor at Bridge House on Wayside Street; a lump of granite was hollowed out and filled with vinegar into which coins were dropped in the belief they would be sanitised so allowing money to buy goods to change hands.

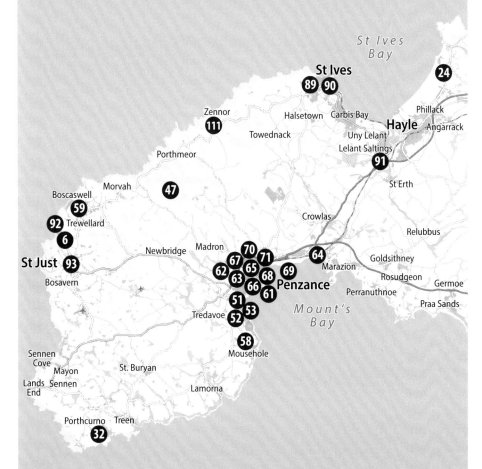

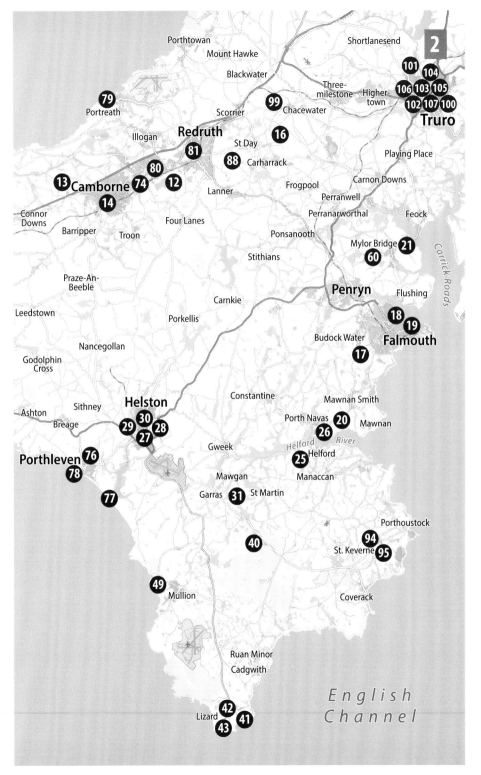

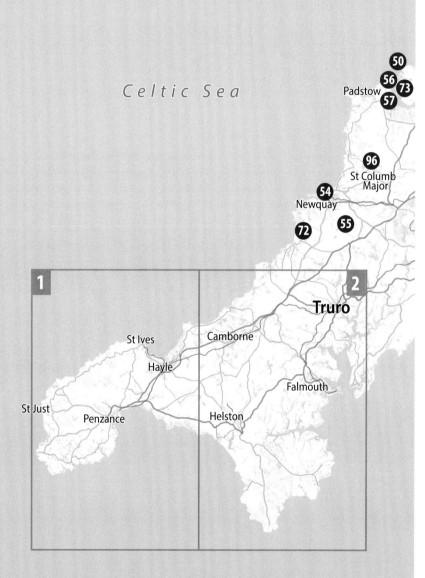

3

Celtic Sea

50

56 **73**

Padstow

57

96

St Columb
Major

54

Newquay

72

55

1

2

St Ives

Camborne

Truro

Hayle

Falmouth

St Just

Penzance

Helston

English Channel

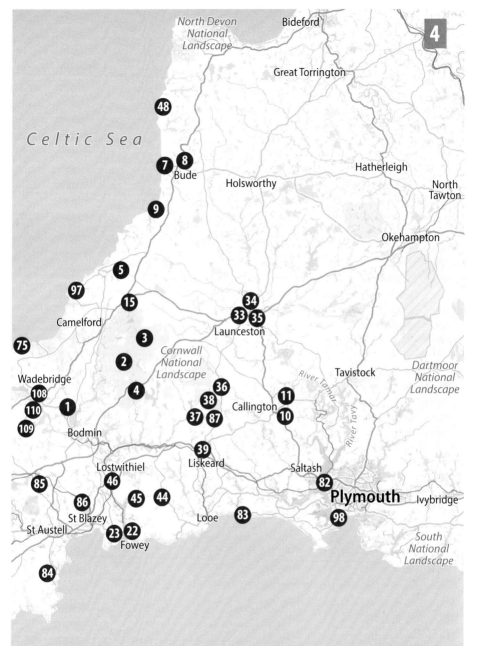

Ed Glinert, David Taylor
**111 Places in Yorkshire
That You Shouldn't Miss**
ISBN 978-3-7408-1167-9

Ed Glinert, Karin Tearle
**111 Places in Essex
That You Shouldn't Miss**
ISBN 978-3-7408-1593-6

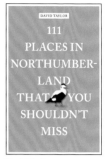

David Taylor
**111 Places in Northumberland
That You Shouldn't Miss**
ISBN 978-3-7408-1792-3

Ed Glinert, David Taylor
**111 Places in Oxford
That You Shouldn't Miss**
ISBN 978-3-7408-1990-3

Solange Berchemin,
Martin Dunford, Karin Tearle
**111 Places in Greenwich
That You Shouldn't Miss**
ISBN 978-3-7408-1107-5

John Sykes, Birgit Weber
**111 Places in London
That You Shouldn't Miss**
ISBN 978-3-7408-1644-5

David Taylor
**111 Places in Newcastle
That You Shouldn't Miss**
ISBN 978-3-7408-1043-6

David Taylor
**111 Places along Hadrian's
Wall That You Shouldn't Miss**
ISBN 978-3-7408-1425-0

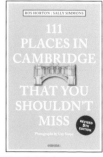

Rosalind Horton,
Sally Simmons, Guy Snape
**111 Places in Cambridge
That You Shouldn't Miss**
ISBN 978-3-7408-1285-0

Phil Lee, Rachel Ghent
**111 Places in Nottingham
That You Shouldn't Miss**
ISBN 978-3-7408-2261-3

Ben Waddington, Janet Hart
**111 Places in Birmingham
That You Shouldn't Miss**
ISBN 978-3-7408-2268-2

Solange Berchemin
**111 Places in the Lake District
That You Shouldn't Miss**
ISBN 978-3-7408-1861-6

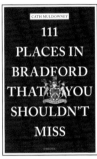

Cath Muldowney
**111 Places in Bradford
That You Shouldn't Miss**
ISBN 978-3-7408-1427-4

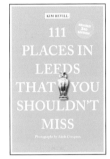

Kim Revill, Alesh Compton
**111 Places in Leeds
That You Shouldn't Miss**
ISBN 978-3-7408-0754-2

Michael Glover,
Richard Anderson
**111 Places in Sheffield
That You Shouldn't Miss**
ISBN 978-3-7408-2348-1

Julian Treuherz,
Peter de Figueiredo
**111 Places in Manchester
That You Shouldn't Miss**
ISBN 978-3-7408-2246-0

Julian Treuherz,
Peter de Figueiredo
**111 Places in Liverpool
That You Shouldn't Miss**
ISBN 978-3-7408-1607-0

Katherine Bebo, Oliver Smith
**111 Places in Poole
That You Shouldn't Miss**
ISBN 978-3-7408-0598-2

Katherine Bebo, Oliver Smith
111 Places in Bournemouth
That You Shouldn't Miss
ISBN 978-3-7408-1166-2

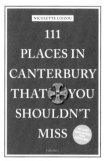

Nicolette Loizou
111 Places in Canterbury
That You Shouldn't Miss
ISBN 978-3-7408-0899-0

Rob Ganley, Ian Williams
111 Places in Coventry
That You Shouldn't Miss
ISBN 978-3-7408-1044-3

Martin Booth, Barbara Evripidou
111 Places in Bristol
That You Shouldn't Miss
ISBN 978-3-7408-2001-5

Martin Booth, Barbara Evripidou
111 Places for Kids in Bristol
That You Shouldn't Miss
ISBN 978-3-7408-1665-0

Alexandra Loske
111 Places in Brighton and
Lewes That You Shouldn't Miss
ISBN 978-3-7408-1727-5

Justin Postlethwaite
111 Places in Bath
That You Shouldn't Miss
ISBN 978-3-7408-0146-5

Gillian Tait
111 Places in Edinburgh
That You Shouldn't Miss
ISBN 978-3-7408-1476-2

Tom Shields, Gillian Tait
111 Places in Glasgow
That You Shouldn't Miss
ISBN 978-3-7408-2237-8